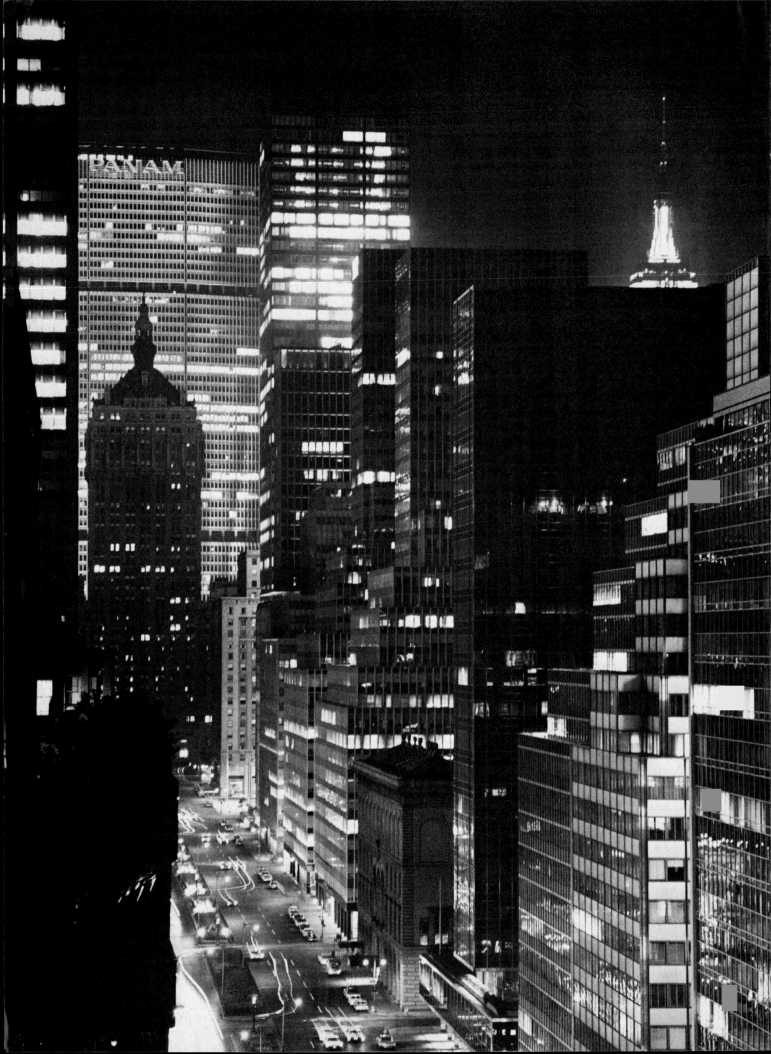

Peter Fink

NEW YORK NOCTURNES

85 After-Dark Photographs

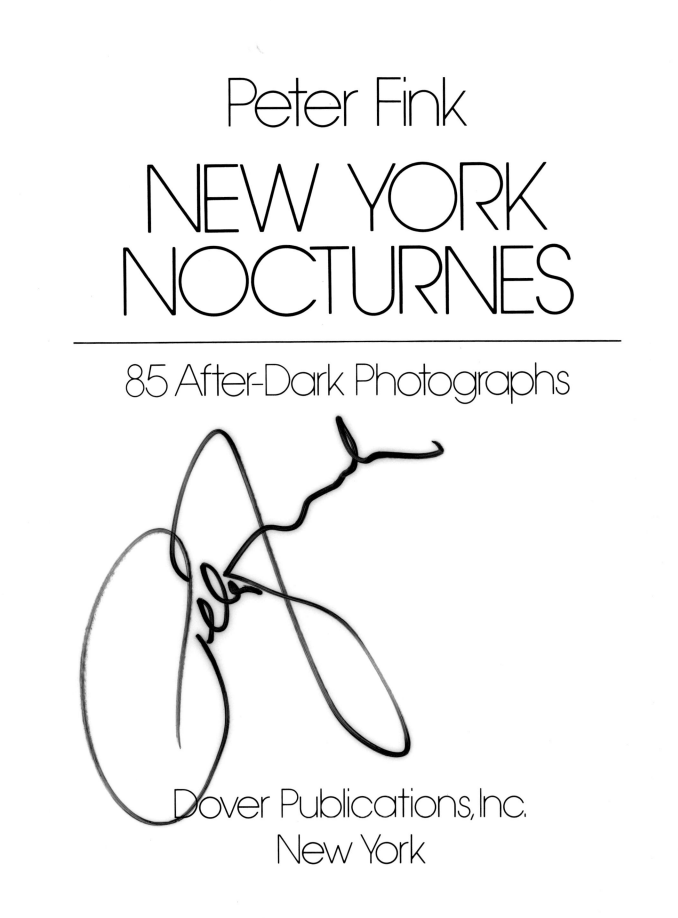

Dover Publications, Inc.
New York

Frontispiece: South on Park Avenue from the upper 50s; the Helmsley Building silhouetted against the Pan Am Building.

Published in Canada by General Publishing Company, Ltd., 30 Lesmill Road, Don Mills, Toronto, Ontario.

Published in the United Kingdom by Constable and Company, Ltd., 10 Orange Street, London WC2H 7EG.

New York Nocturnes: 85 After-Dark Photographs is a new work, first published by Dover Publications, Inc., in 1982.

Manufactured in the United States of America
Dover Publications, Inc.
180 Varick Street
New York, N.Y. 10014

Library of Congress Cataloging in Publication Data

Fink, Peter.
    New York nocturnes.

    1. Photography, Artistic. 2. New York (N.Y.)—
Description—Views. 3. Photography, Night. I. Title.
TR654.F54 1982   779′.997471043   82-1534
ISBN 0-486-24299-4   AACR2

Publisher's Note

The New York that Peter Fink presents to us in this volume is the city of night. The metropolis of seamy daytime reality that New Yorkers know too well and are so widely publicized—the graffiti-marred walls, rusting bridges, raucous noise and jostling crowds—is banished by Mr. Fink's camera. Commonplace objects are metamorphosed and assume lives that are entirely their own. We are invited to wander through a city of dreams, of glowing towers surrounded by a velvety black sky, of parks traversed by shadowy paths echoing soft footfalls, of light-spangled bridges mirrored in jeweled rivers. It is a romantic vision, but one that is as vital to the life of the great city as the iron and concrete of which it is built.

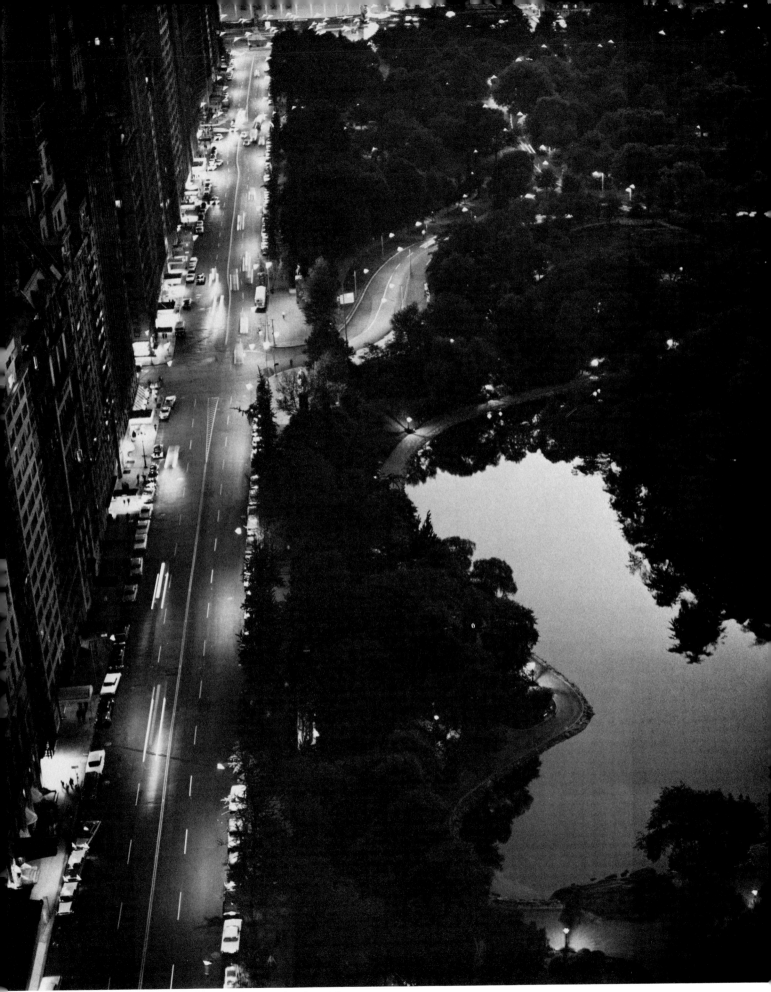

Central Park South west to Columbus Circle; Central Park at right.

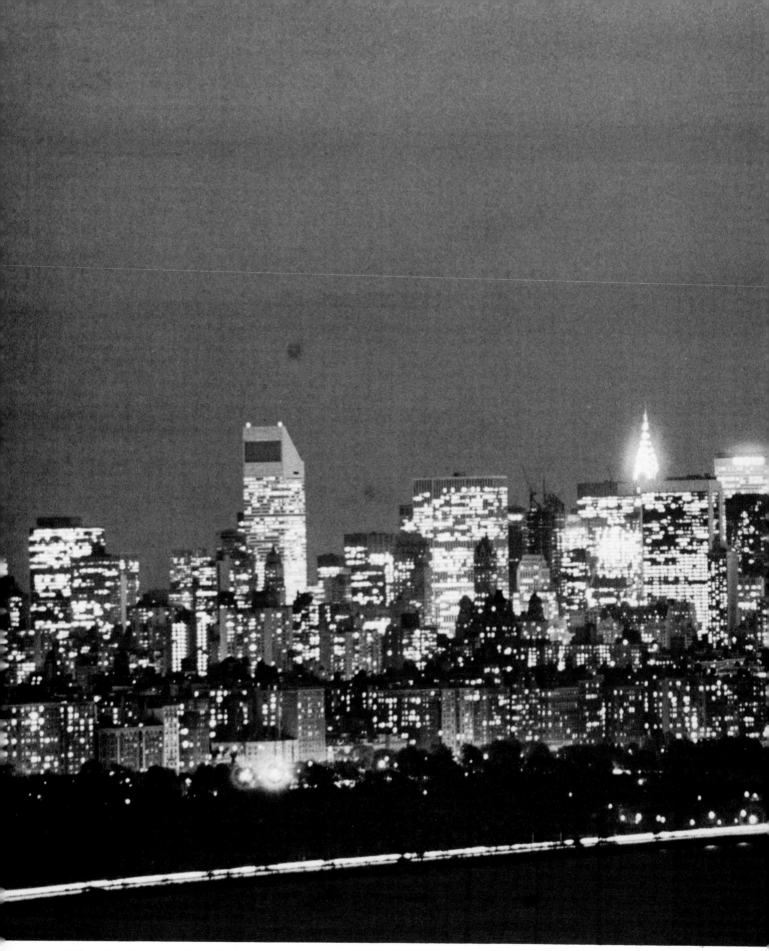

Midtown Manhattan from the Hudson River.

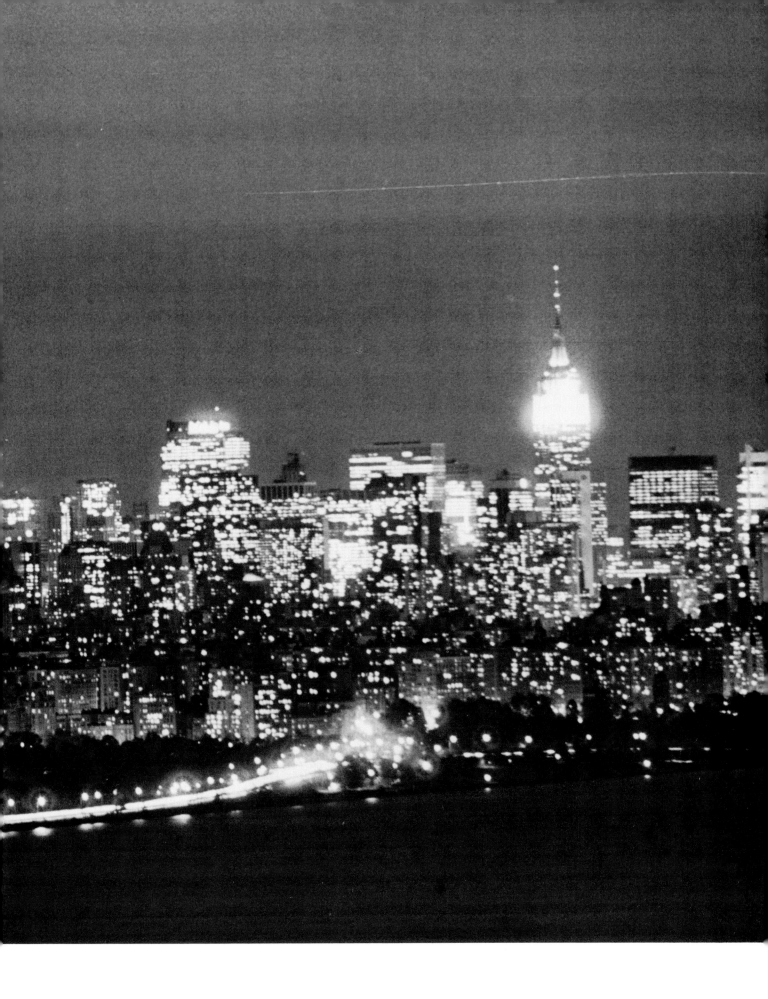

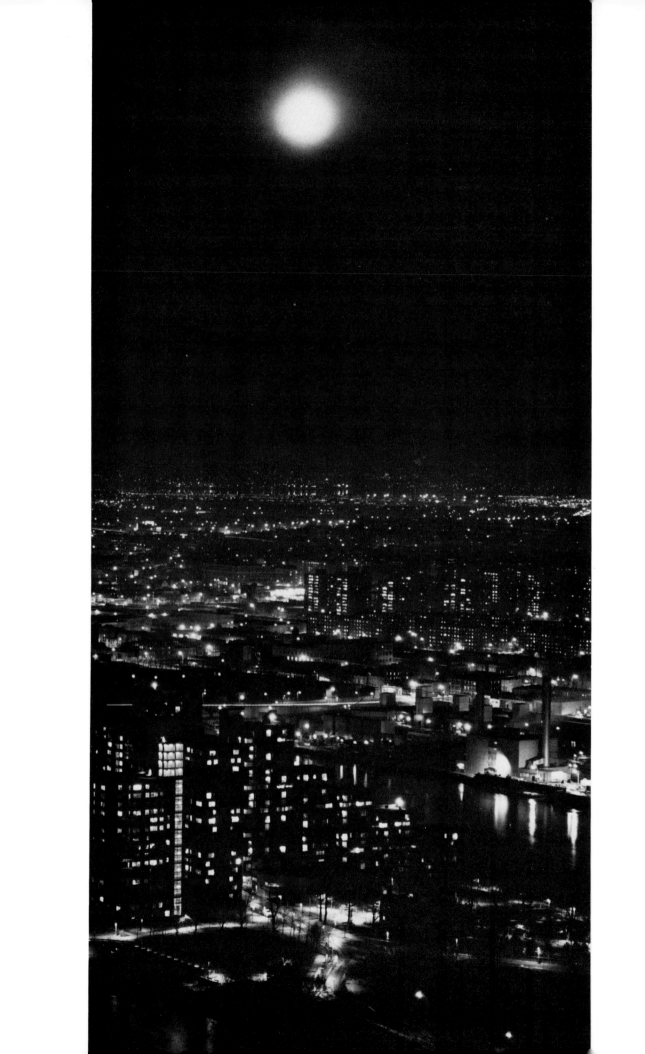

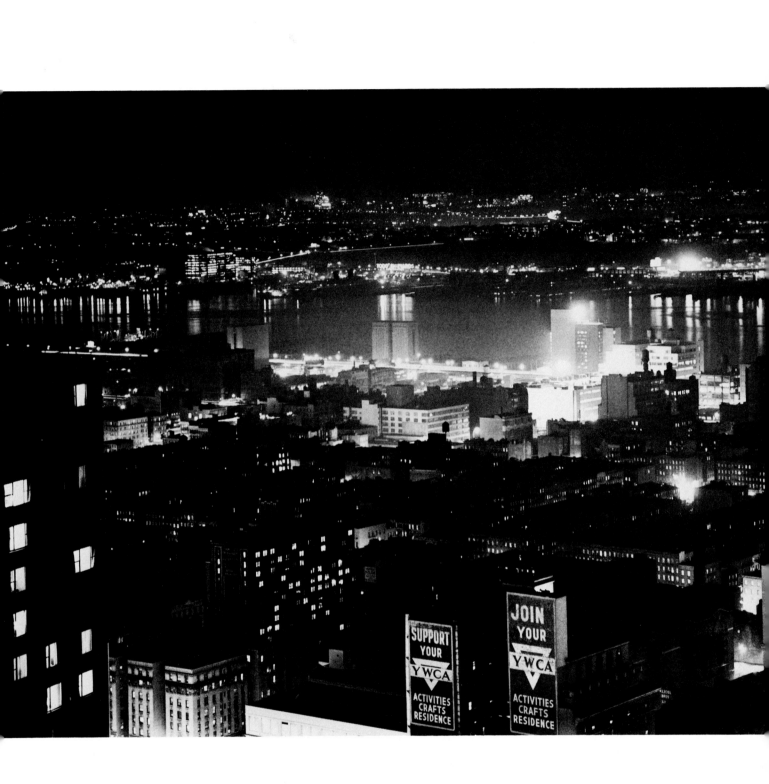

Opposite: Across the East River to Queens; Roosevelt Island at bottom.
Above: Toward the Hudson River from Eighth Avenue and West 50th
Street; the old Madison Square Garden at bottom.
Overleaf: Across the East River to Brooklyn; Williamsburg Bridge at left,
Brooklyn Bridge at right.

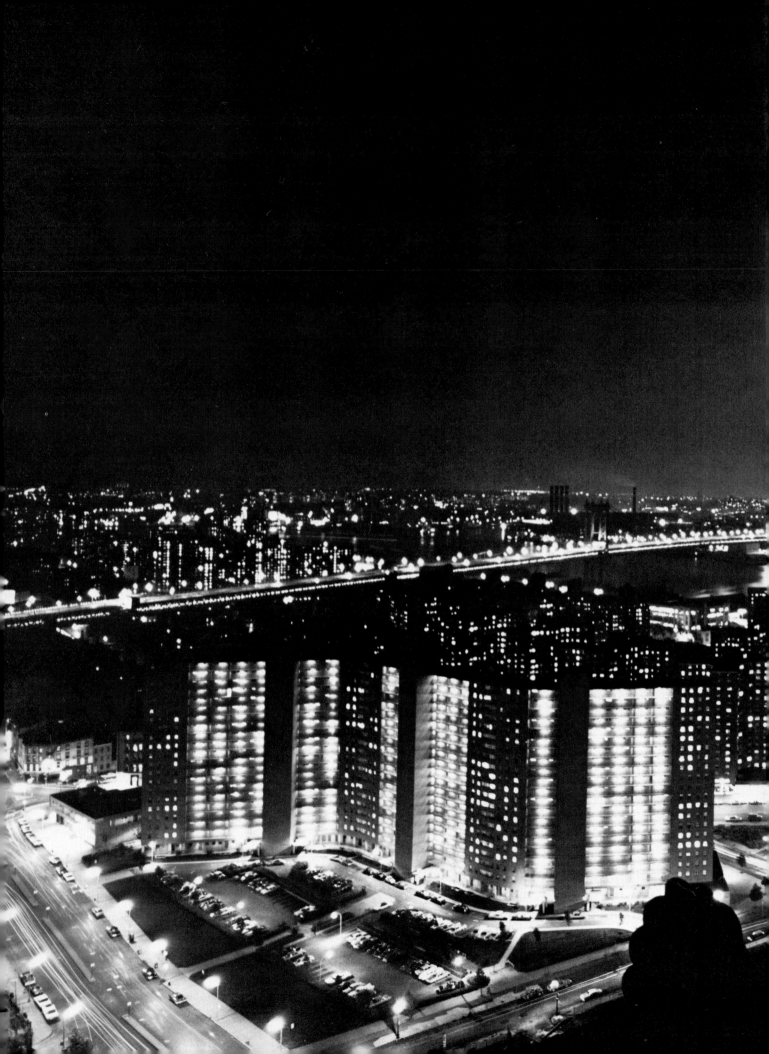

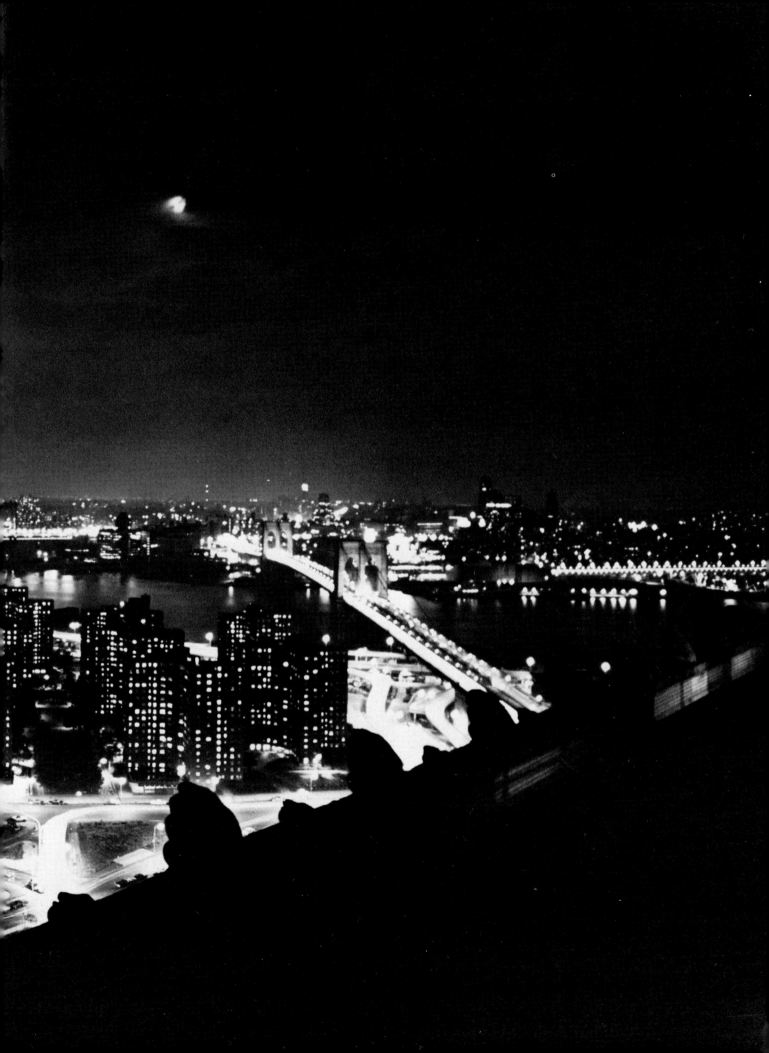

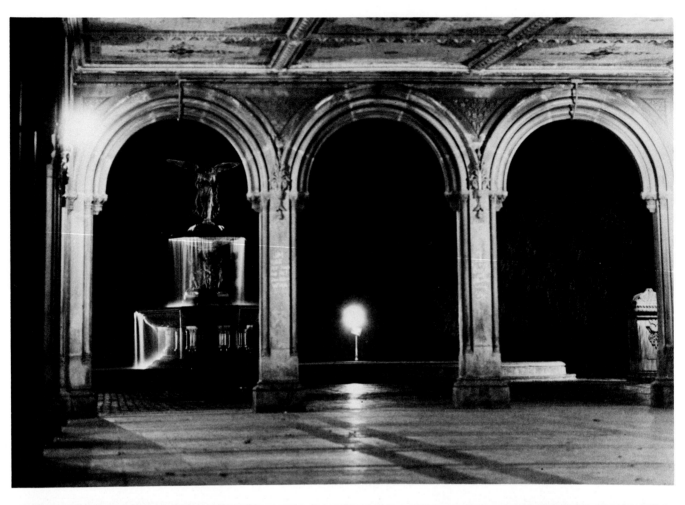

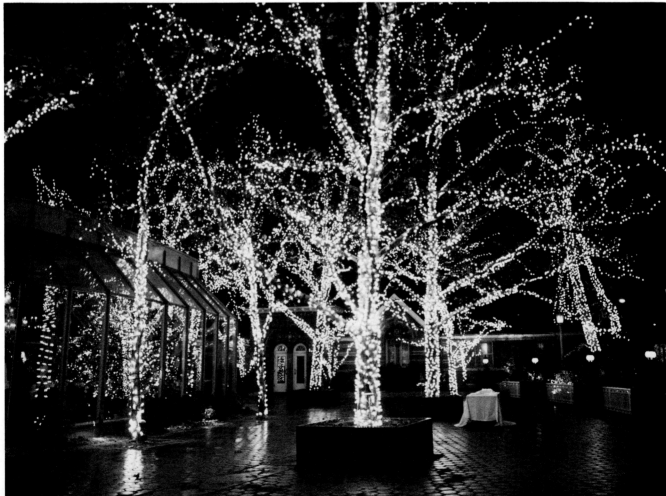

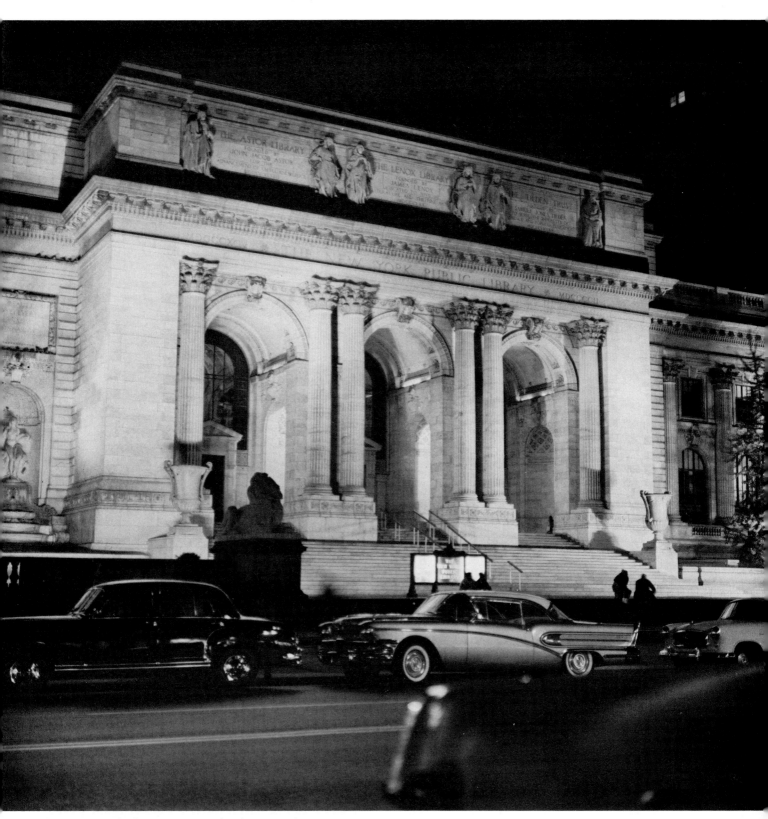

Opposite, top: Bethesda Fountain, Central Park. *Opposite, bottom:* Tavern-on-the-Green, Central Park. *Above:* New York Public Library, Fifth Avenue and West 42nd Street.
Overleaf: Southwest across lower Manhattan from Brooklyn.

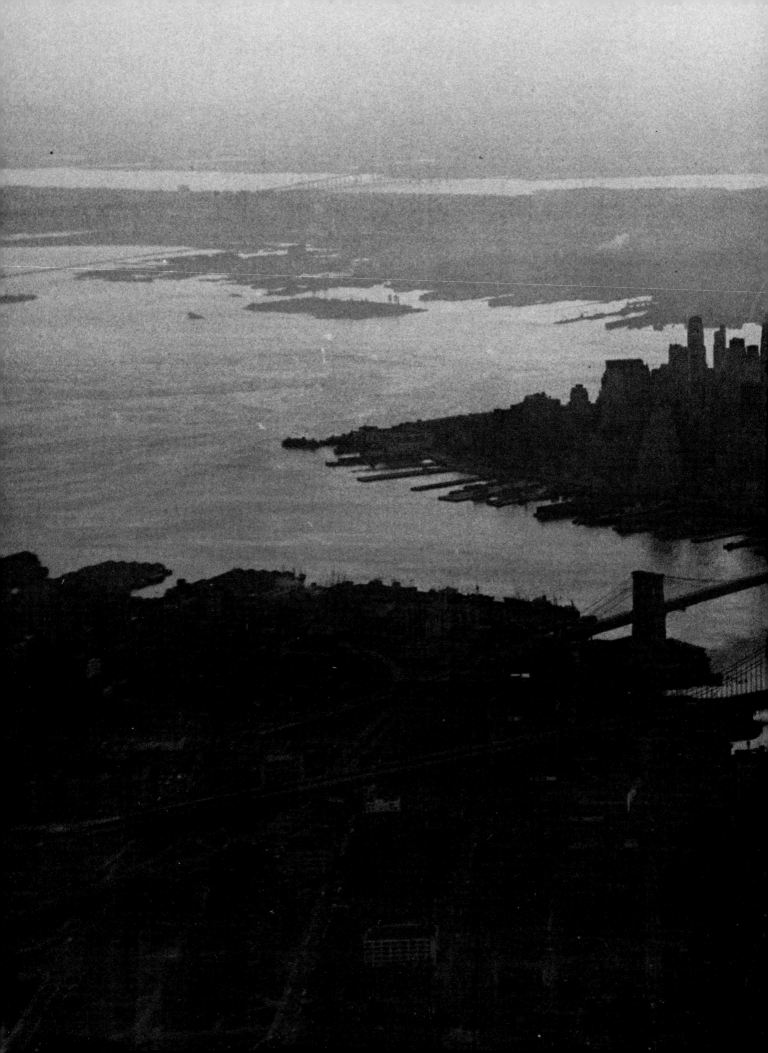

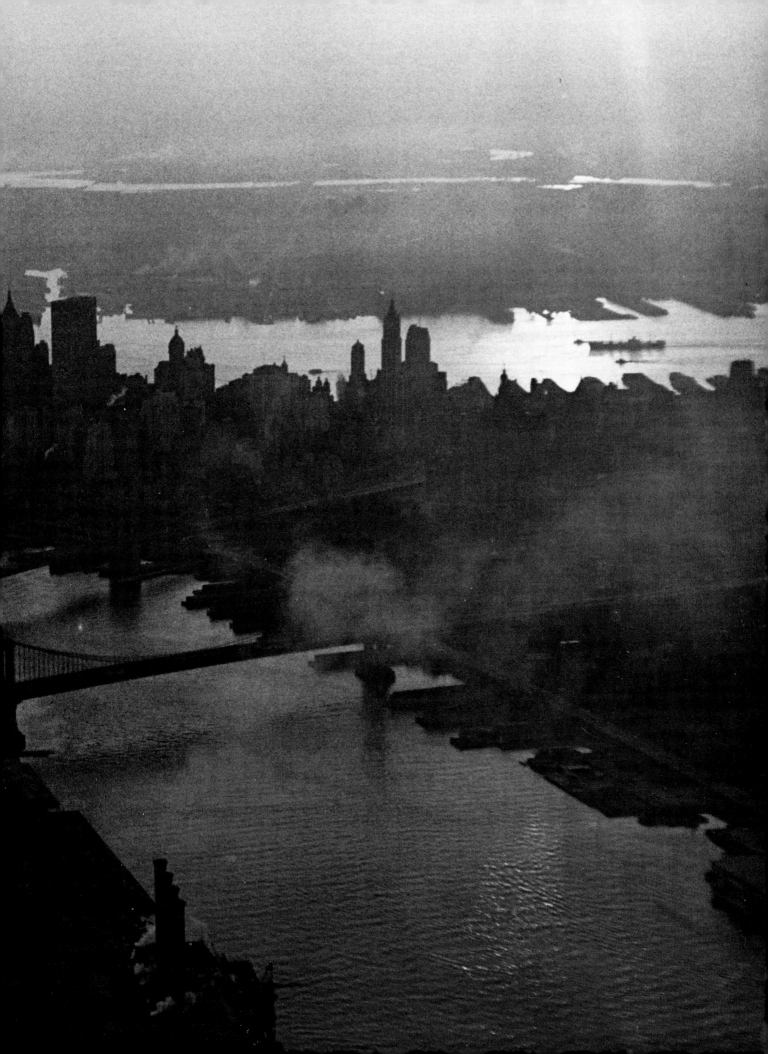

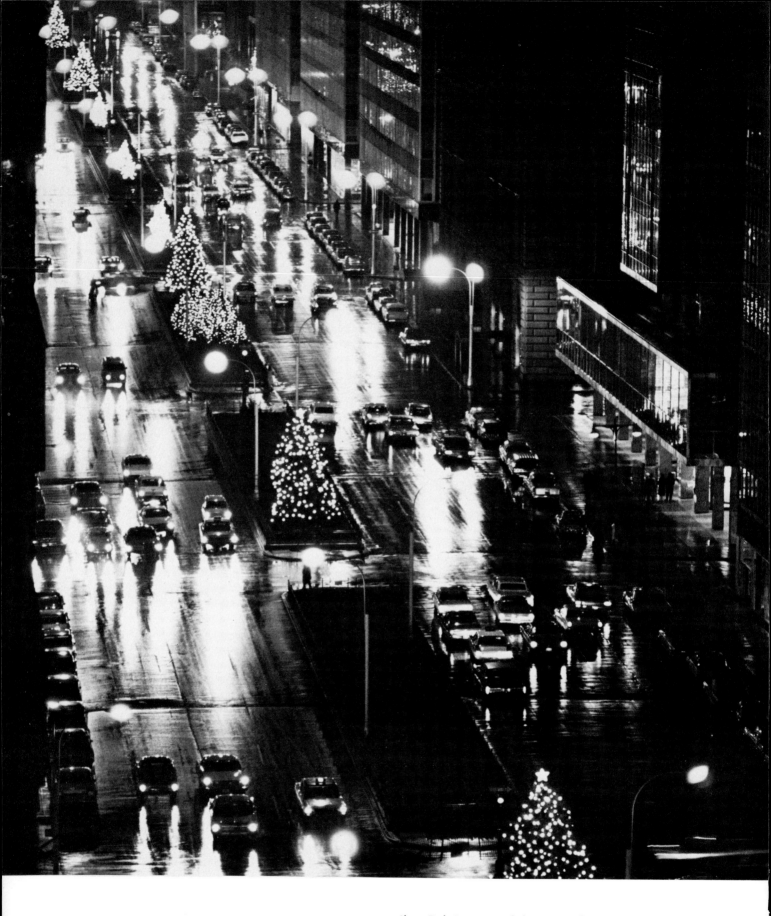

Above: Park Avenue, south from East 55th Street. *Opposite, top:* Central Park West and West 72nd Street. *Opposite, bottom:* Times Square, south from West 48th Street.

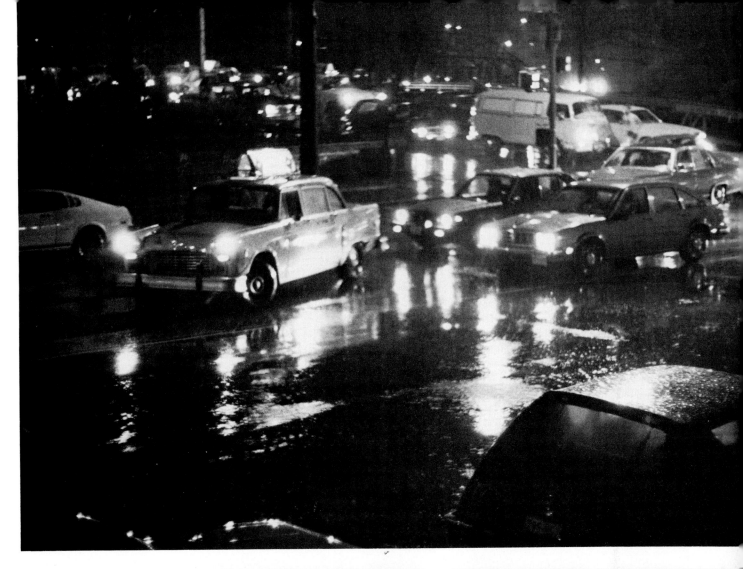

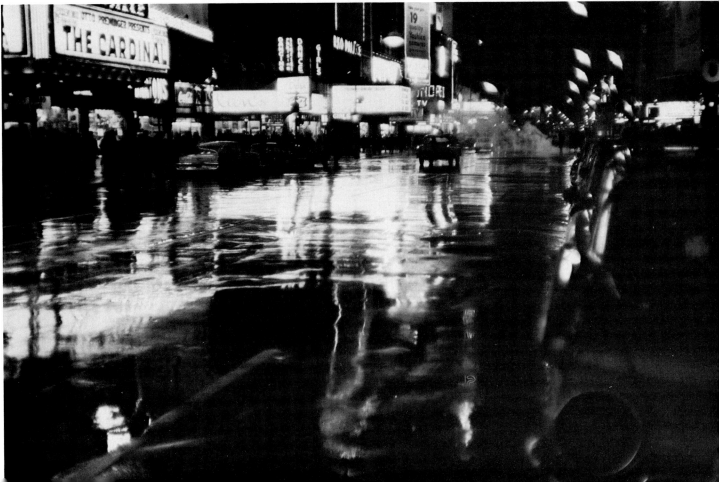

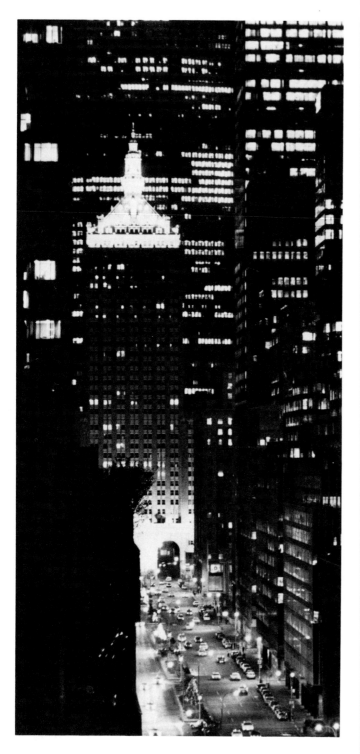

Above: The Helmsley Building, Park Avenue.
Right: The skyline of lower Manhattan from Brooklyn Heights.

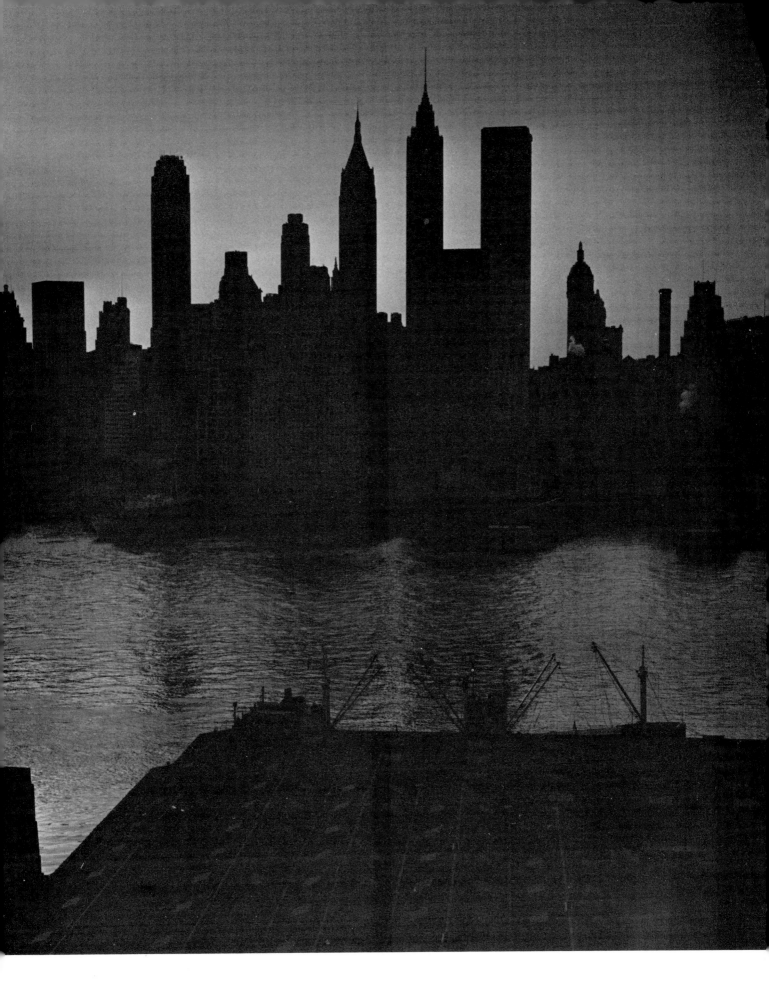

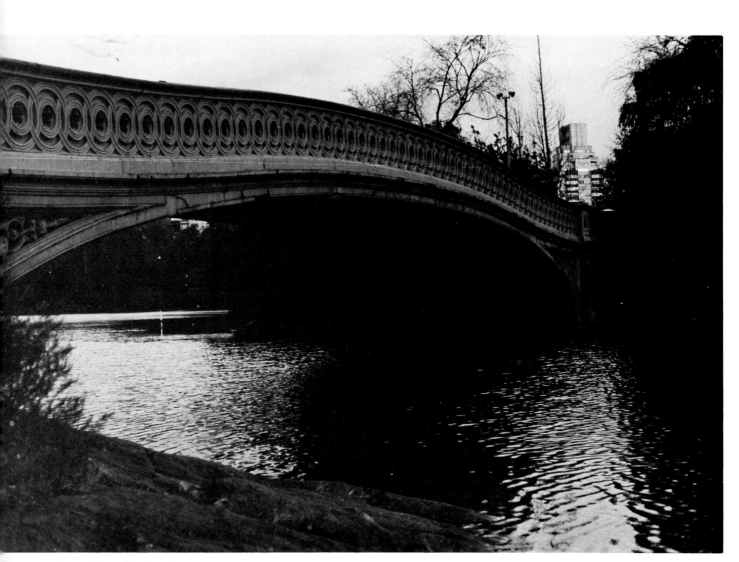

Bow Bridge, Central Park.

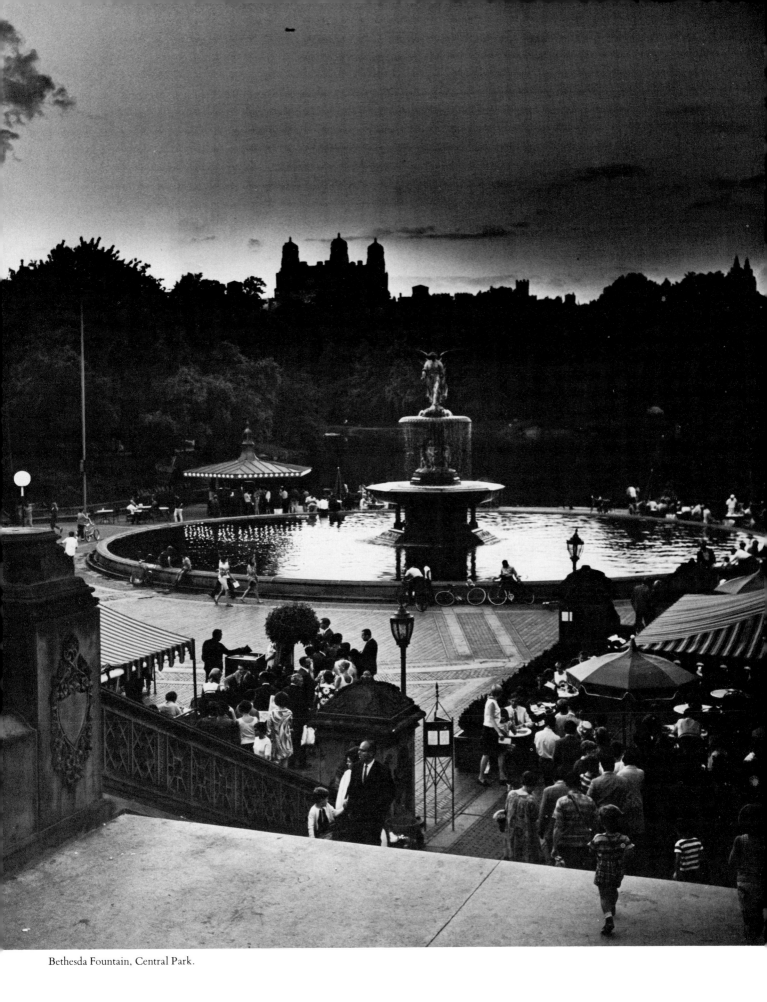

Bethesda Fountain, Central Park.

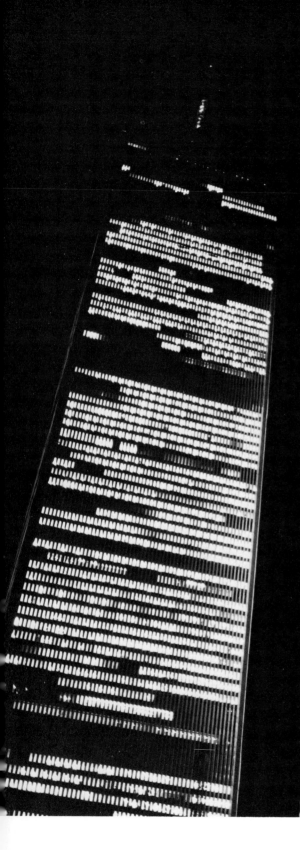

18

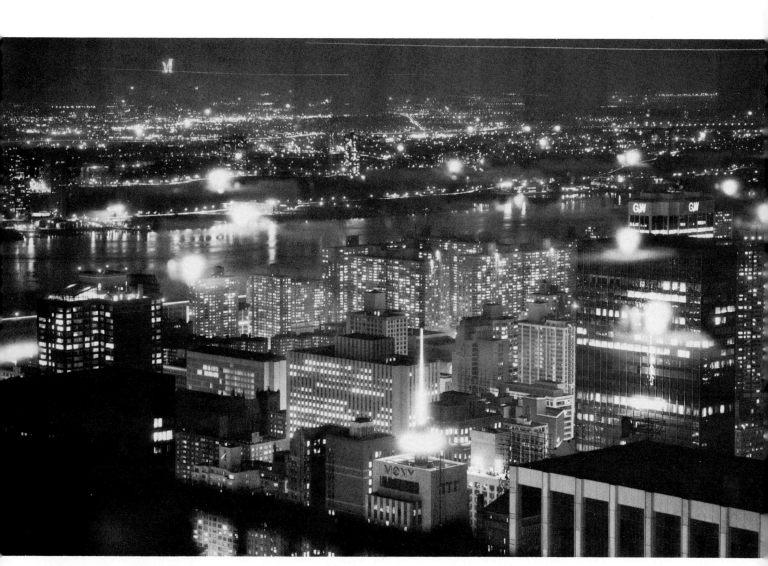

Opposite: The World Trade Center. *Above:* Northwest from the RCA
Building.
Overleaf: Across the Pond toward Central Park South from the Gapstow
Bridge, Central Park.

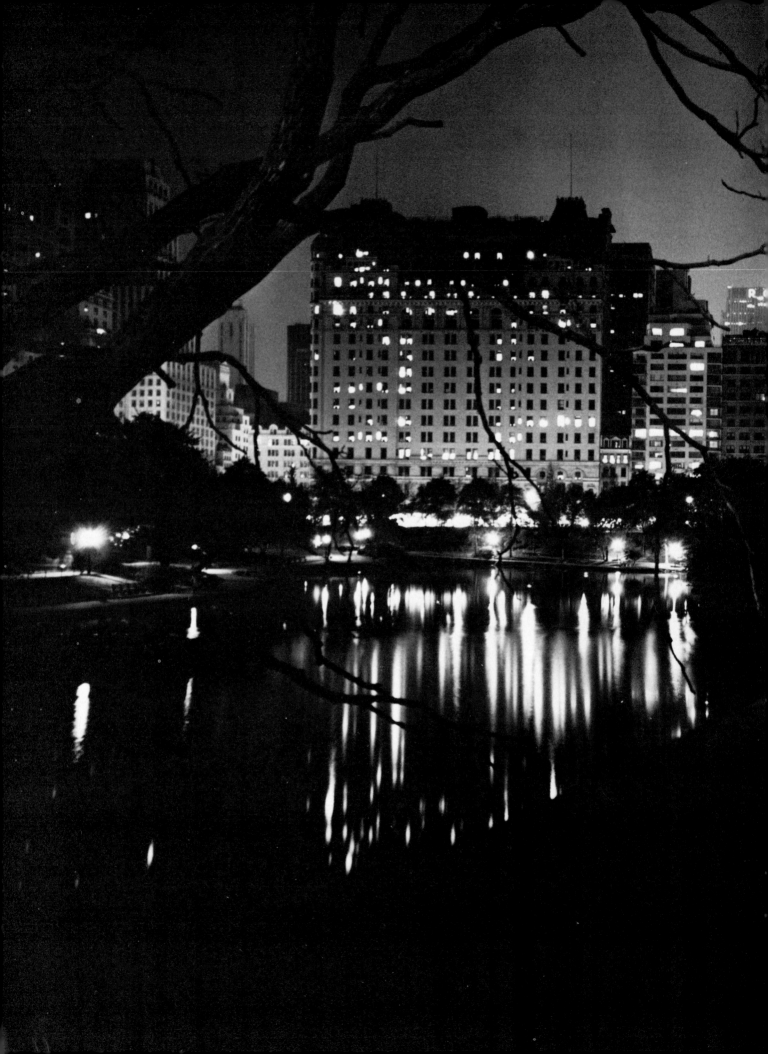

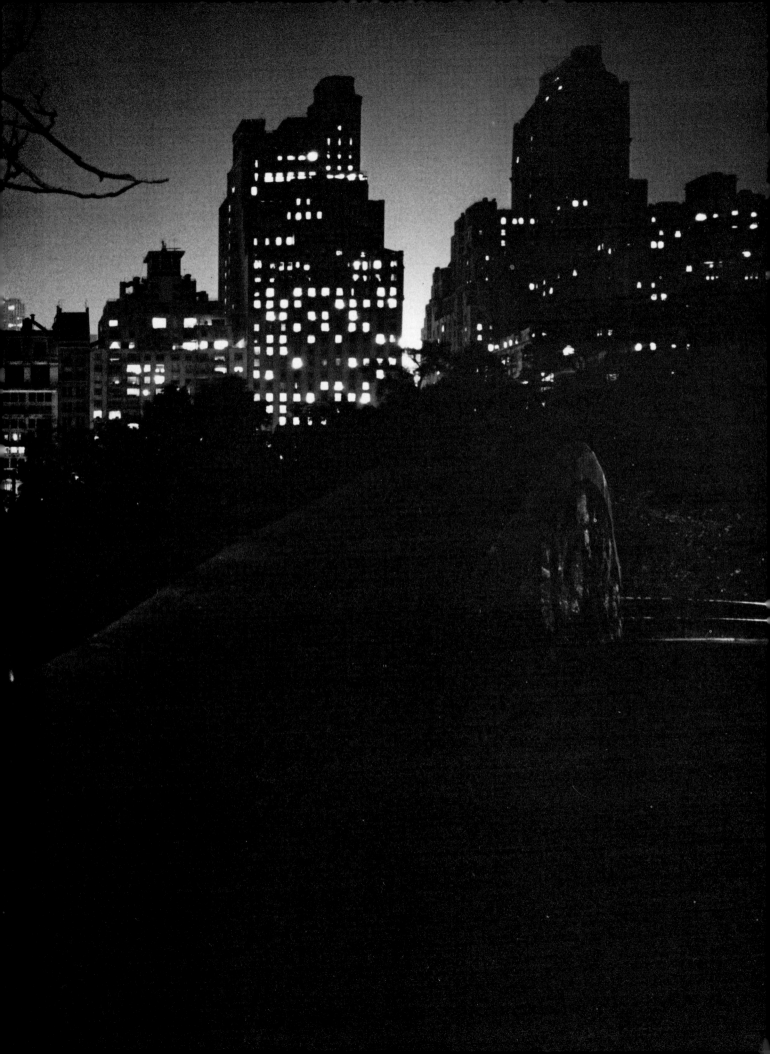

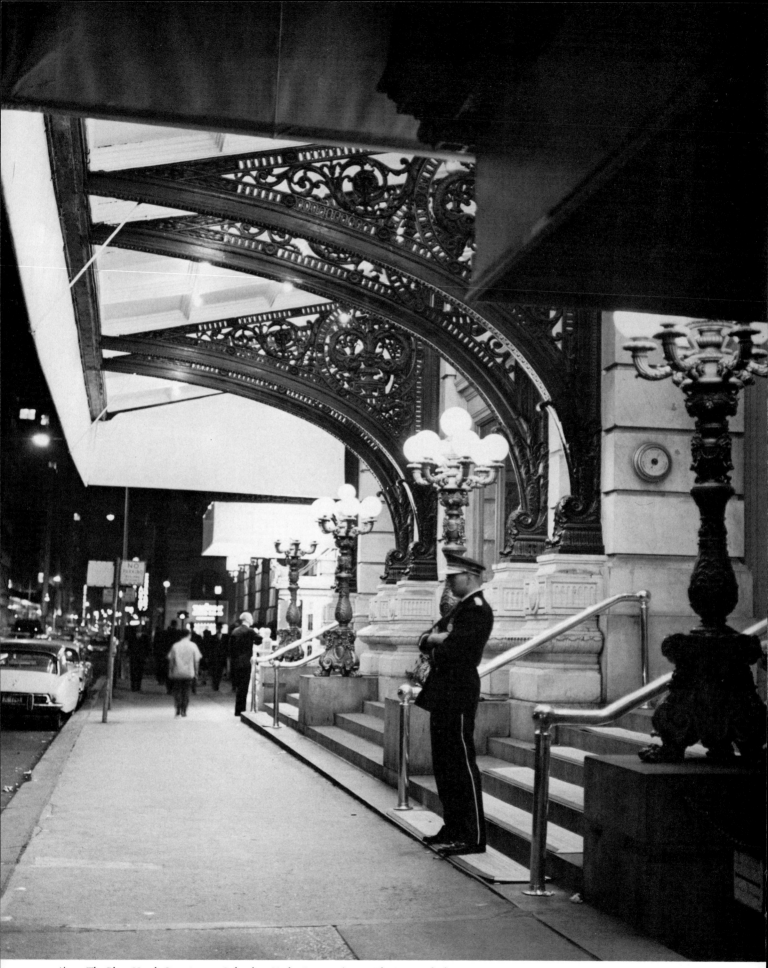

Above: The Plaza Hotel. *Opposite, top:* Columbus Circle. *Opposite, bottom:* The Statue of Liberty.

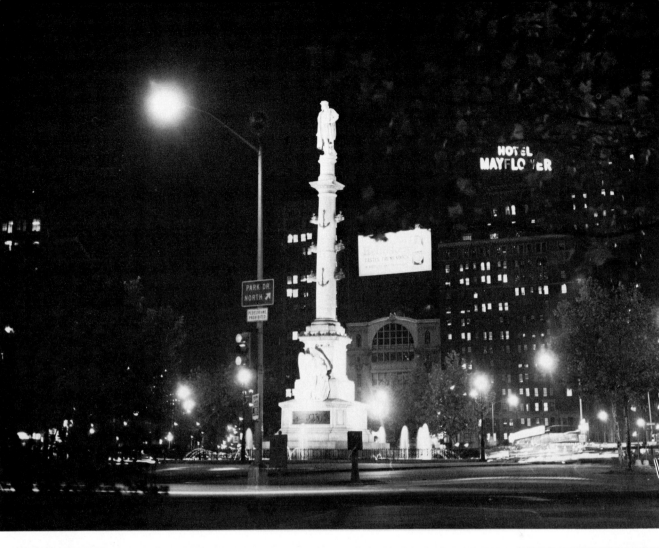

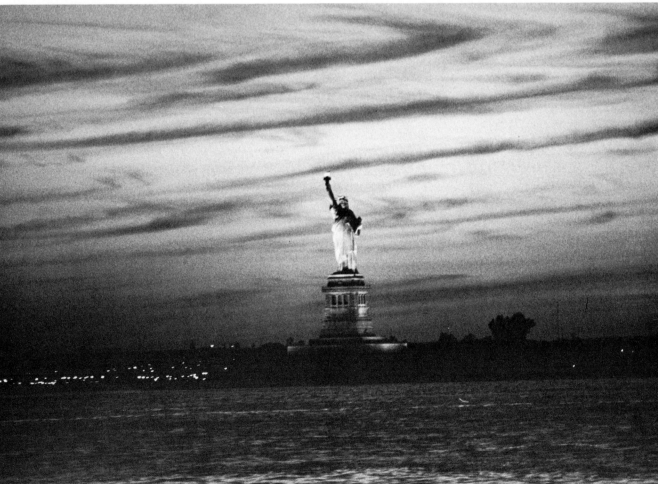

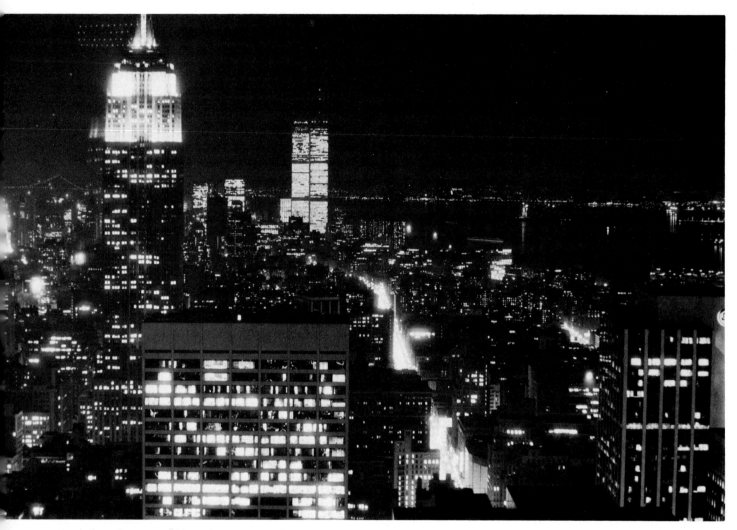

South from the RCA Building; the Empire State Building at left, the
World Trade Center toward center.

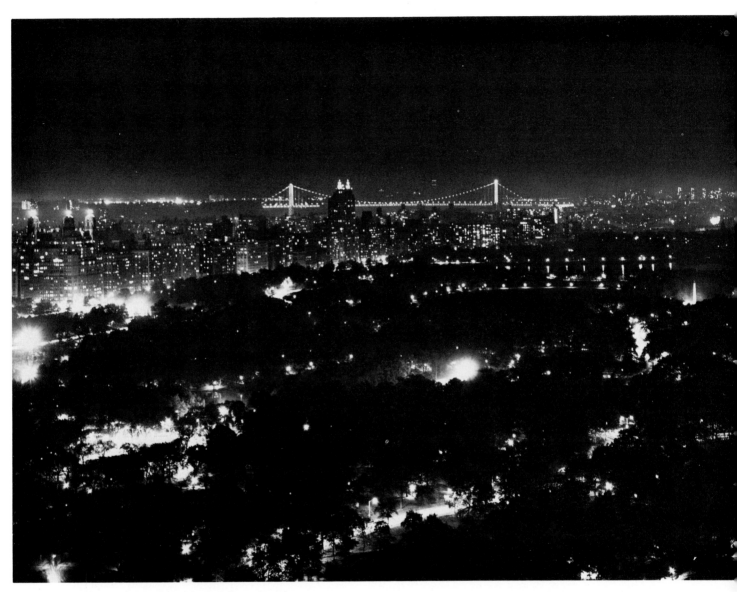

Northwest across Central Park; the George Washington Bridge at center.

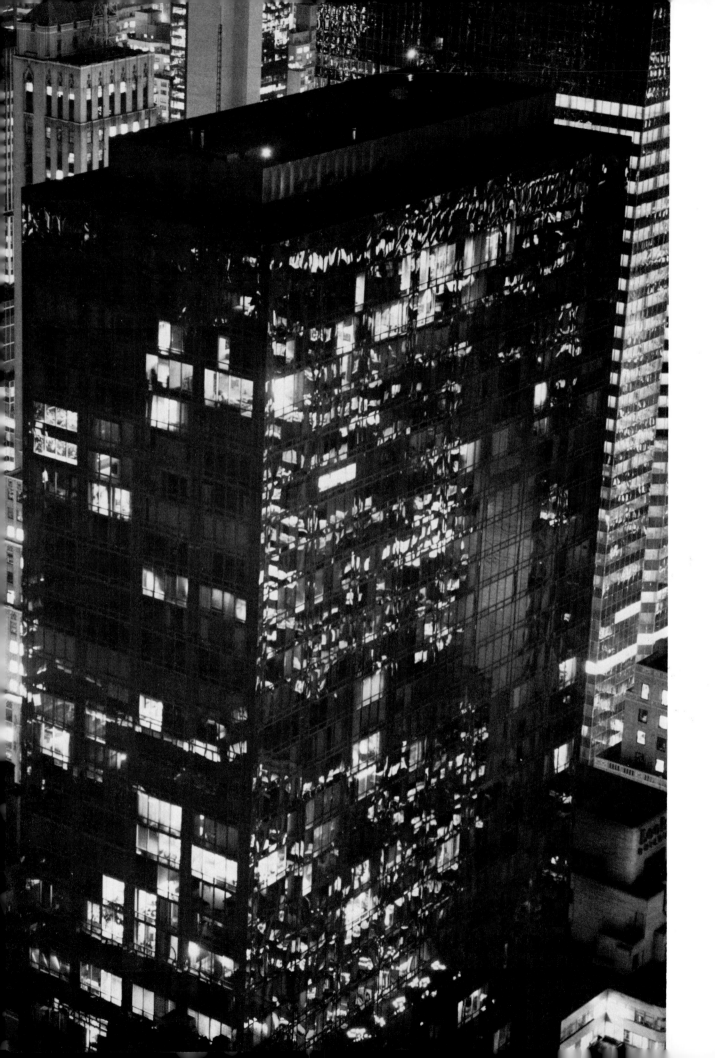

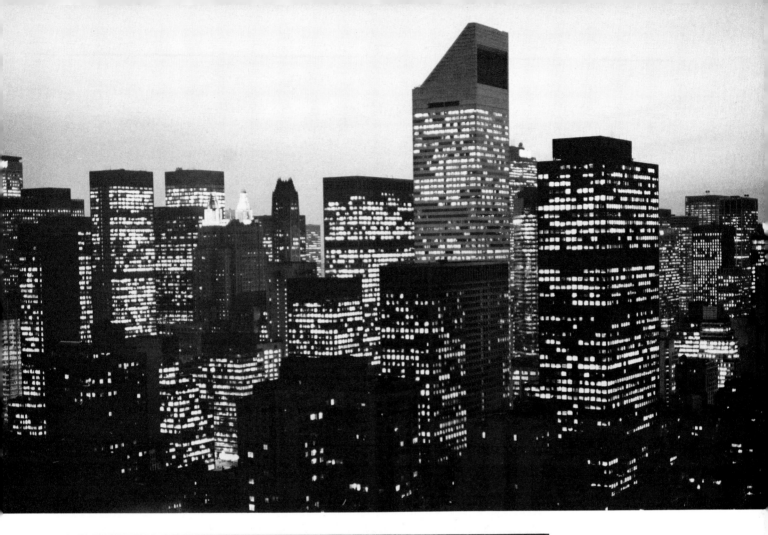

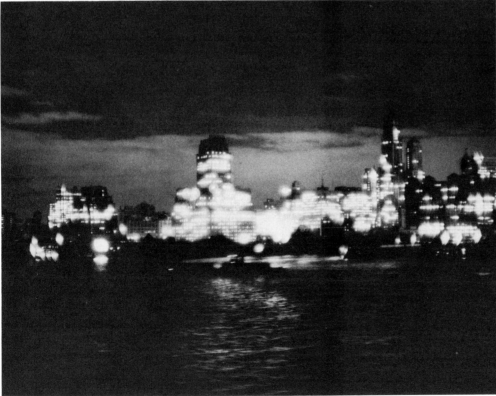

Opposite: The Olympic Tower, Fifth Avenue and East 51st Street.
Top: Southwest from the East 50s; the Citicorp Building at center.
Bottom: Lower Manhattan from the Hudson River.
Overleaf: Southeast across Central Park from the Dakota Apartments,
Central Park West and West 72nd Street.

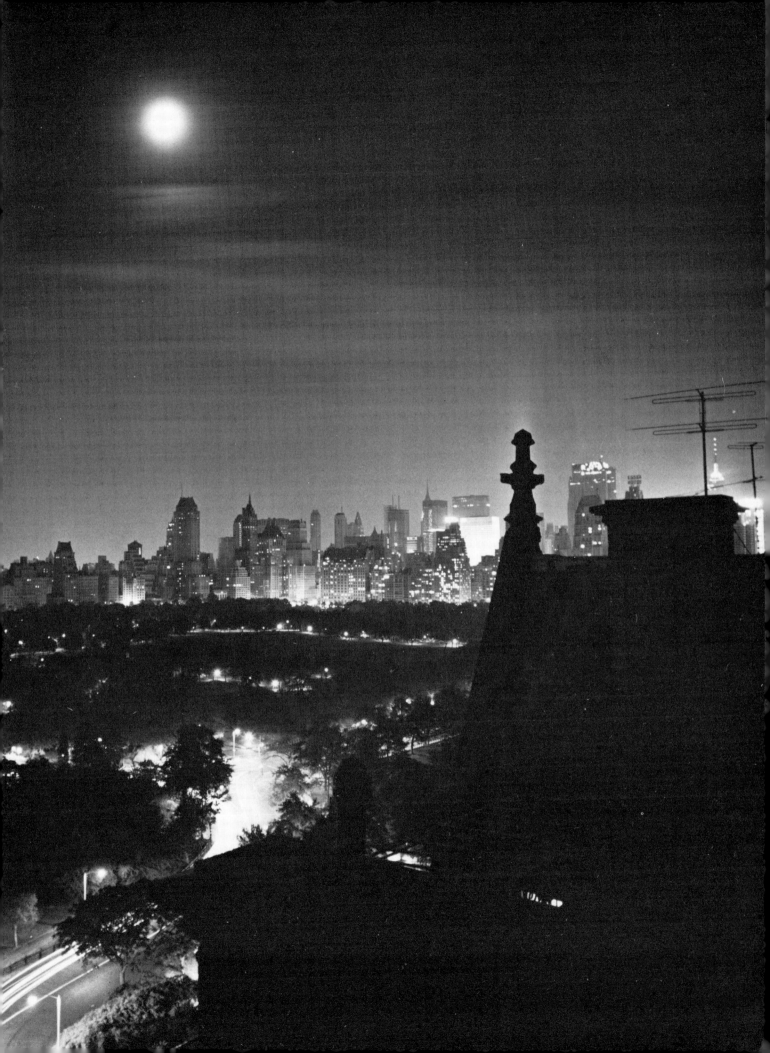

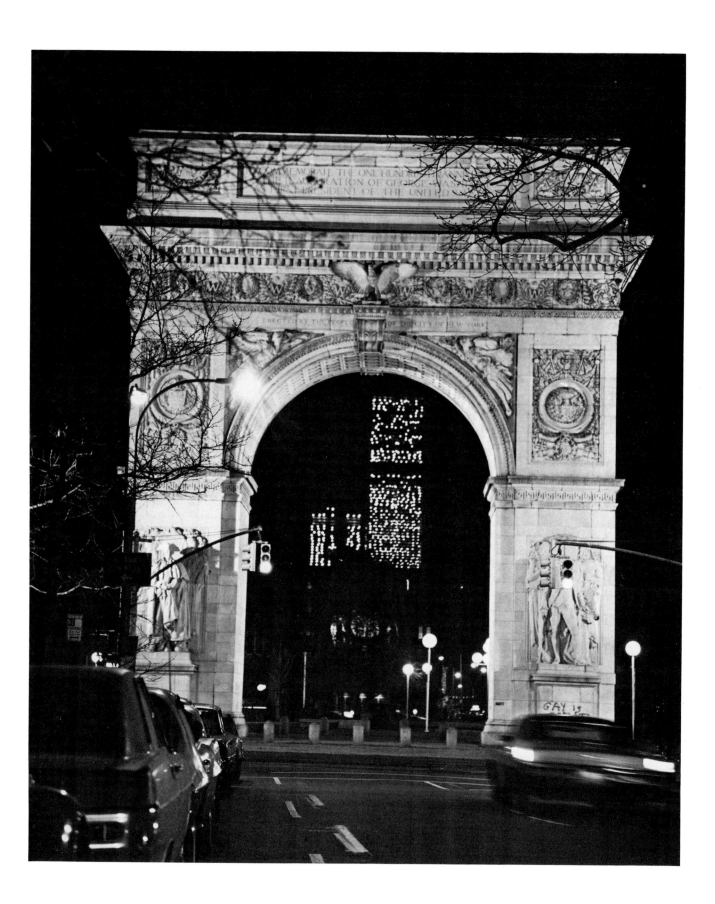

Above: Through the Washington Arch south to the World Trade Center.
Opposite: St. Patrick's Cathedral.

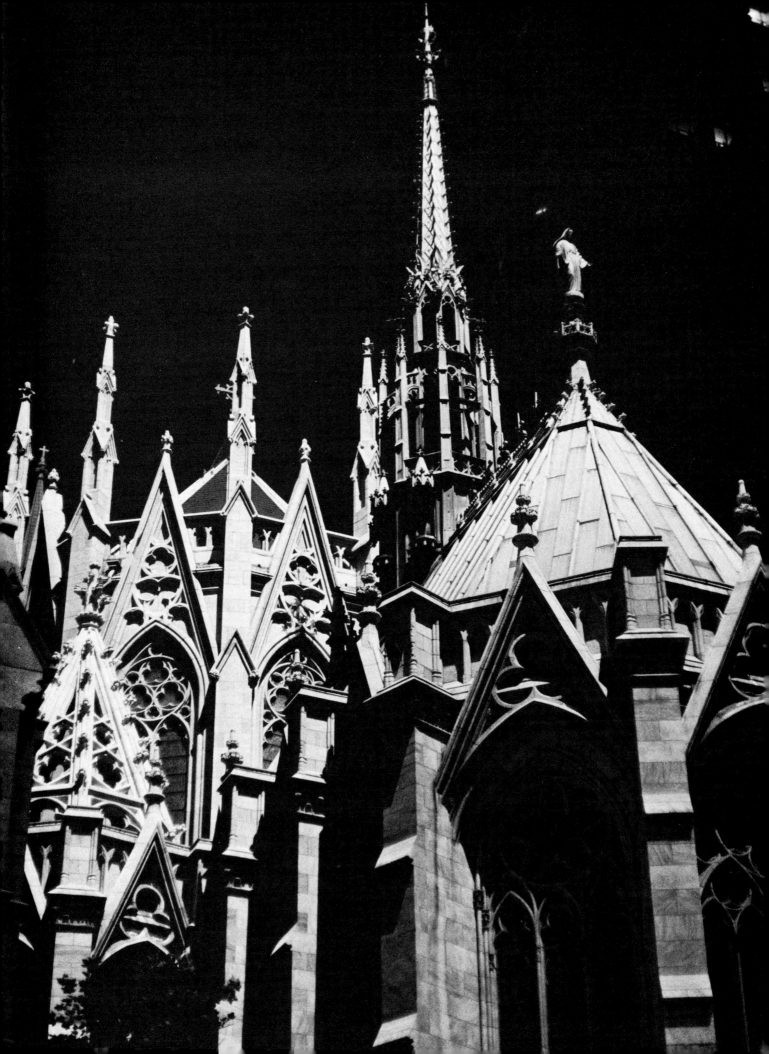

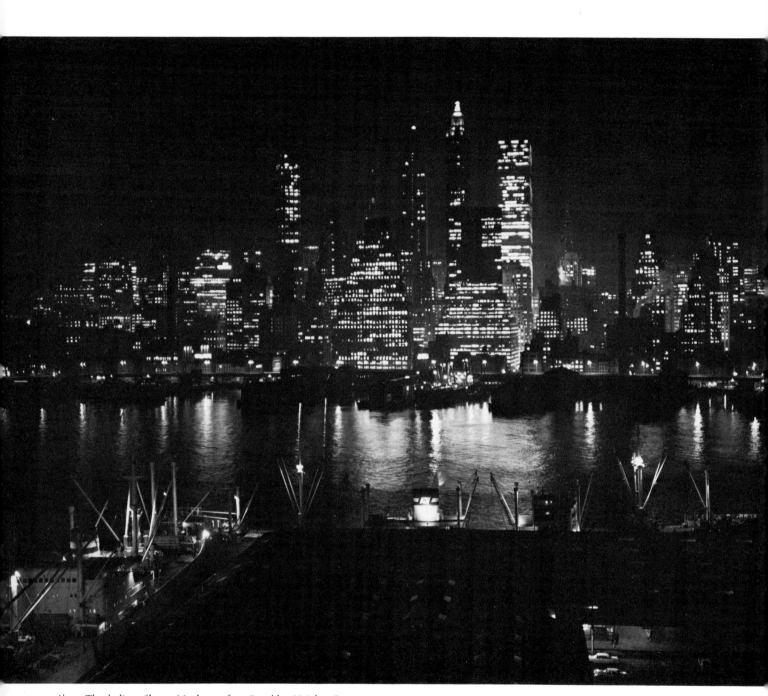

Above: The skyline of lower Manhattan from Brooklyn Heights. *Opposite, top:* South to Central Park South across the Pond, Central Park. *Opposite, bottom:* The skyline of lower Manhattan from Brooklyn Heights.

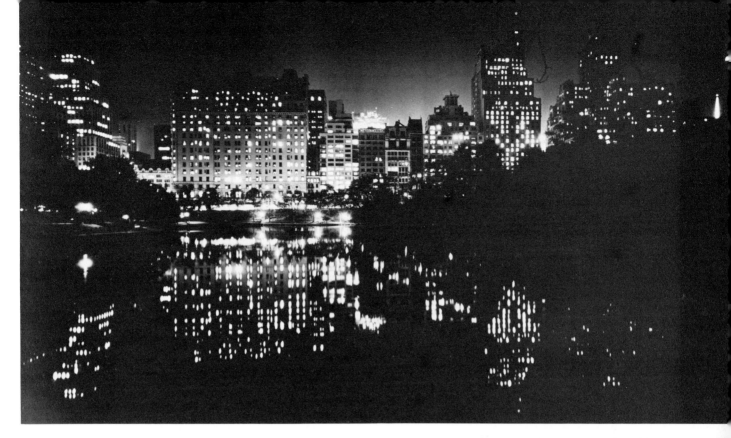

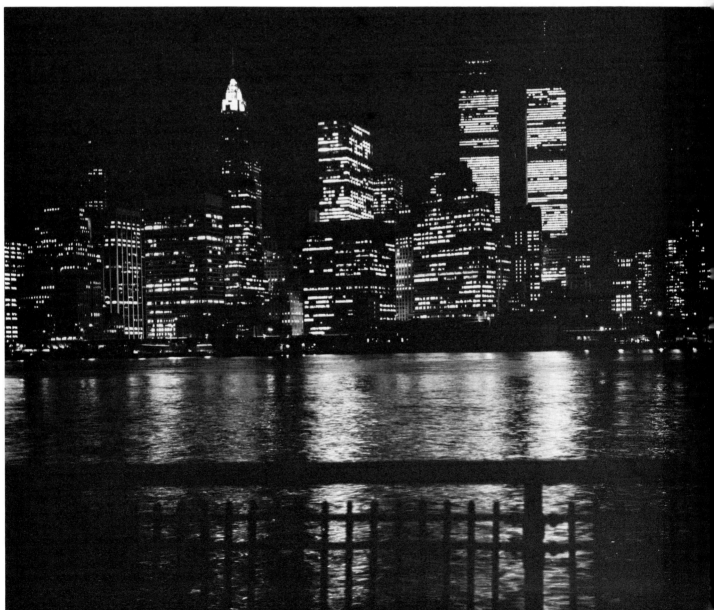

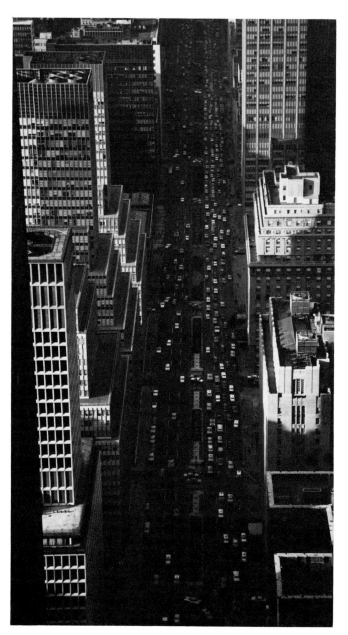

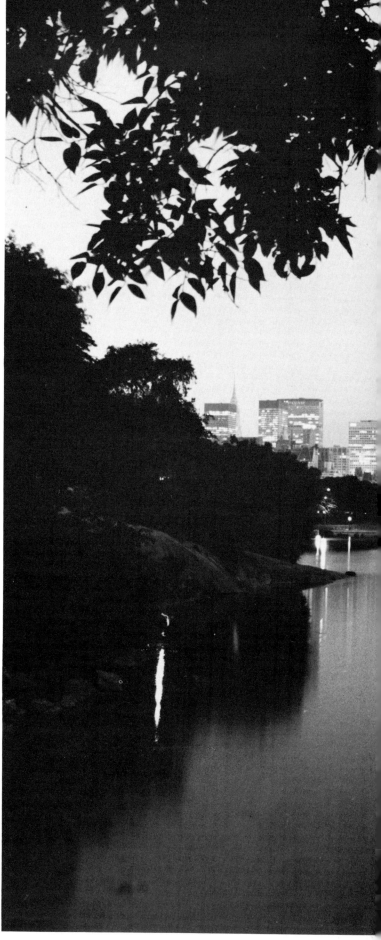

Above: North up Park Avenue in the East 50s. *Right:* Southeast across the Lake from the Bank Rock Bridge, Central Park.

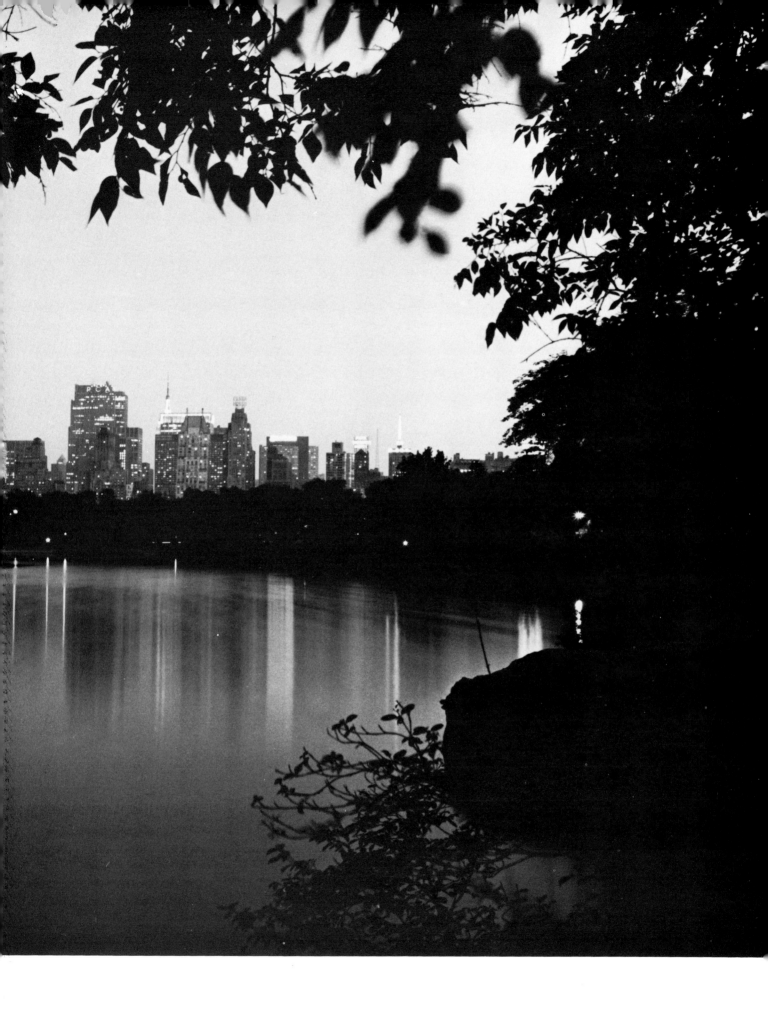

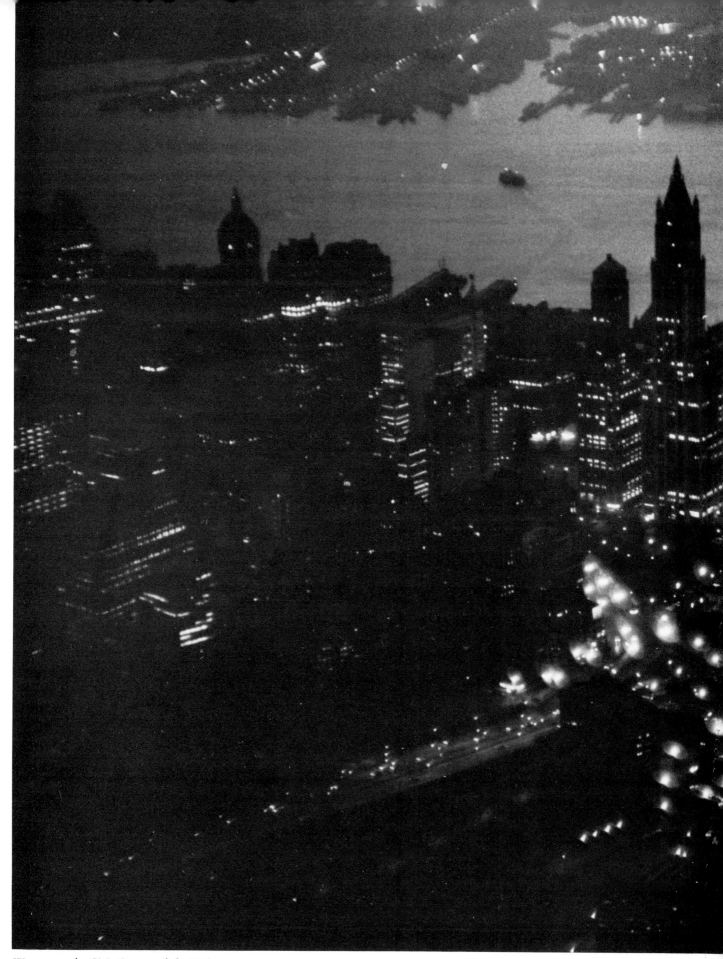

West across the Civic Center and the Hudson River to New Jersey.

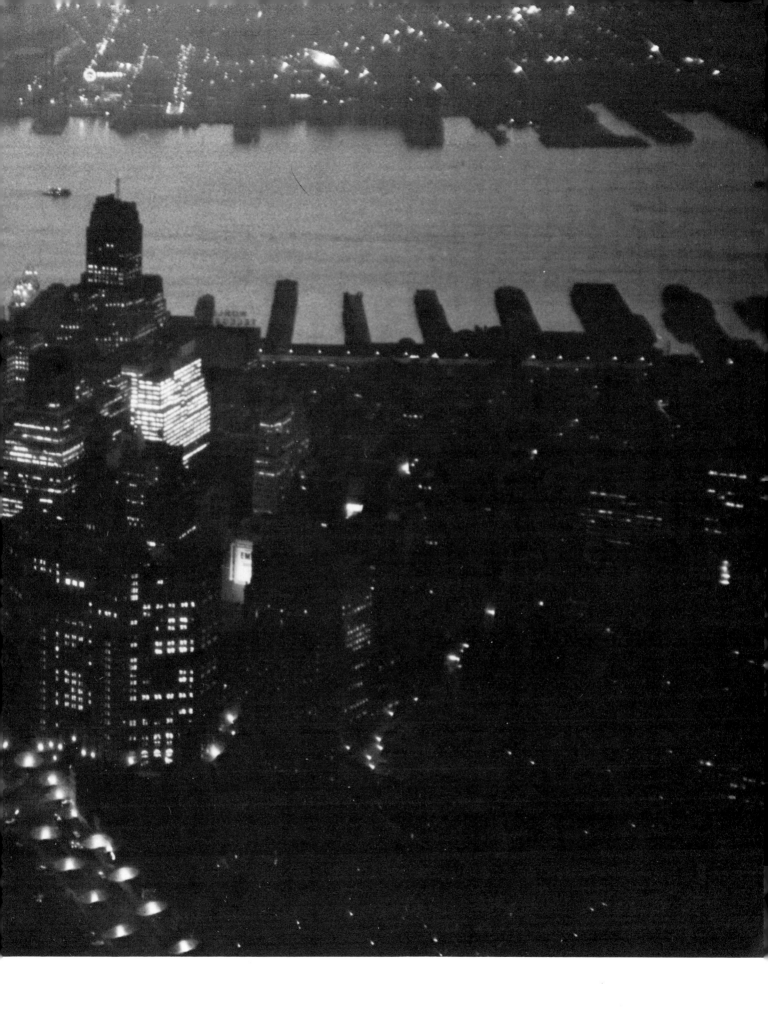

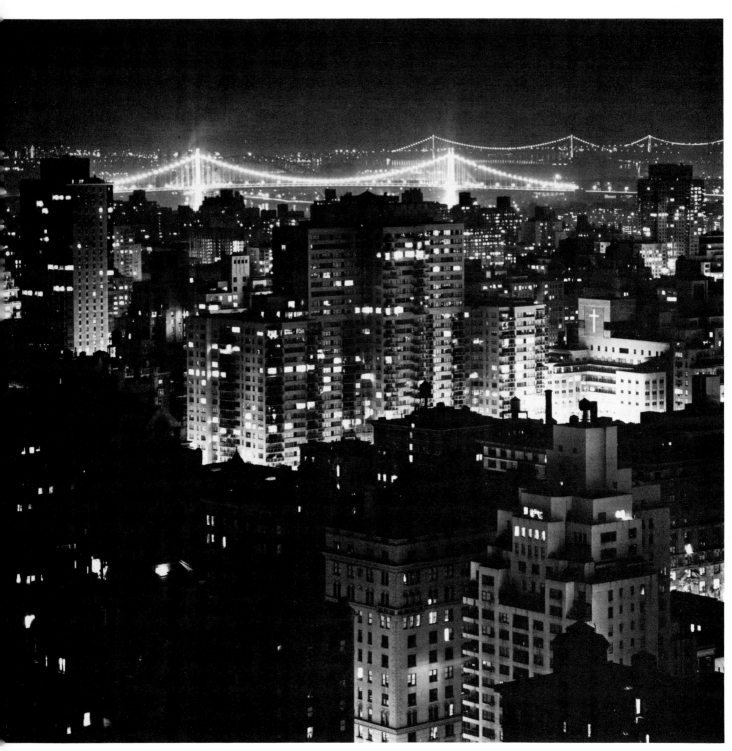

North toward the Triborough Bridge.

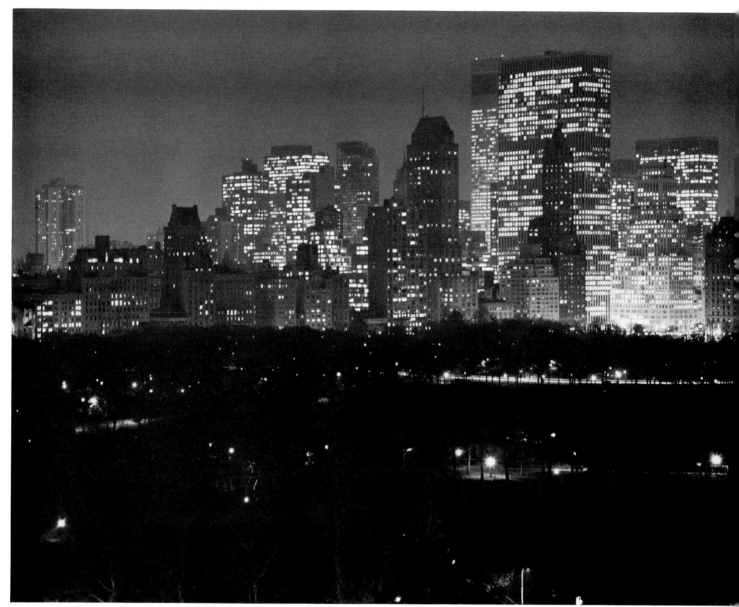

Southeast across Central Park.

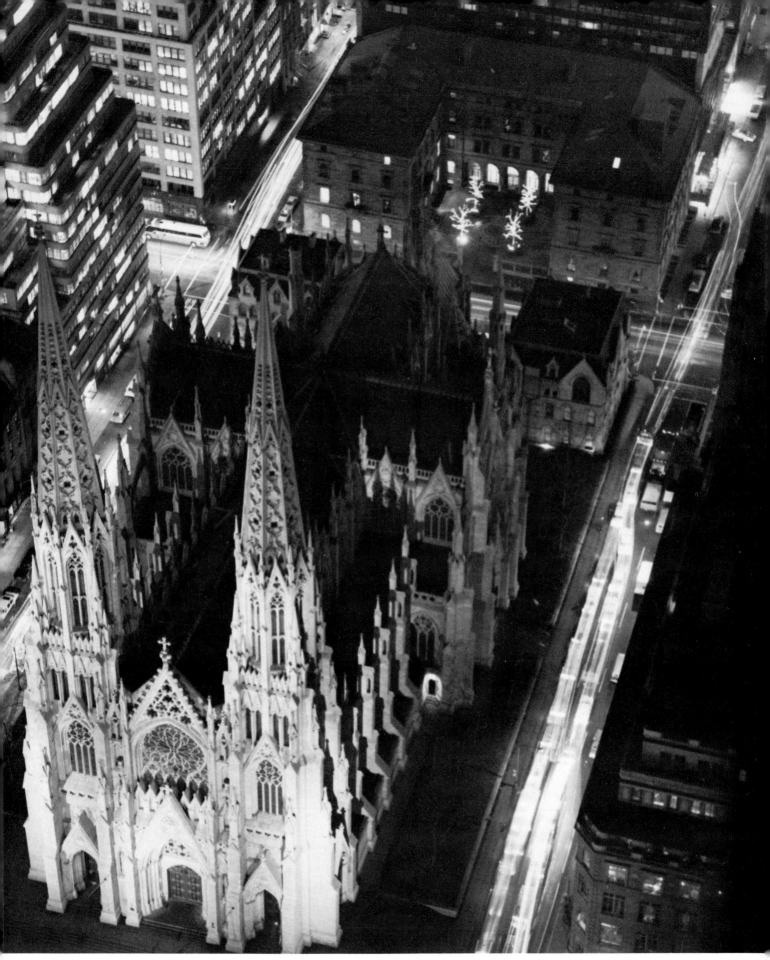

St. Patrick's Cathedral; the Helmsley Palace Hotel behind it.

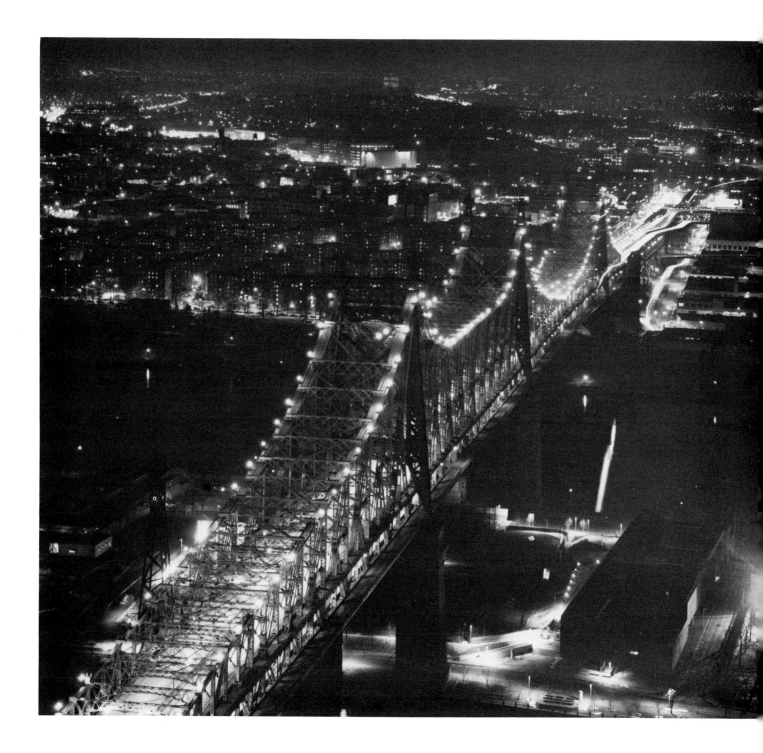

Above: The Queensboro (59th Street) Bridge, East River.
Overleaf: The Queensboro (59th Street) Bridge; Roosevelt Island at center.

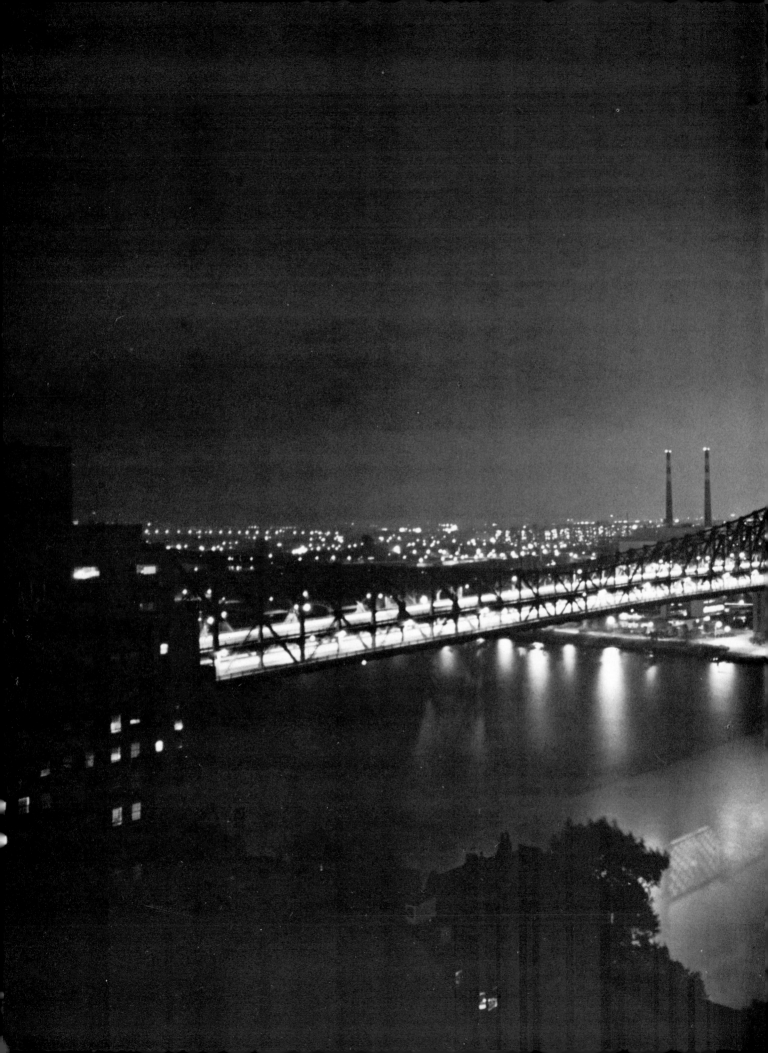

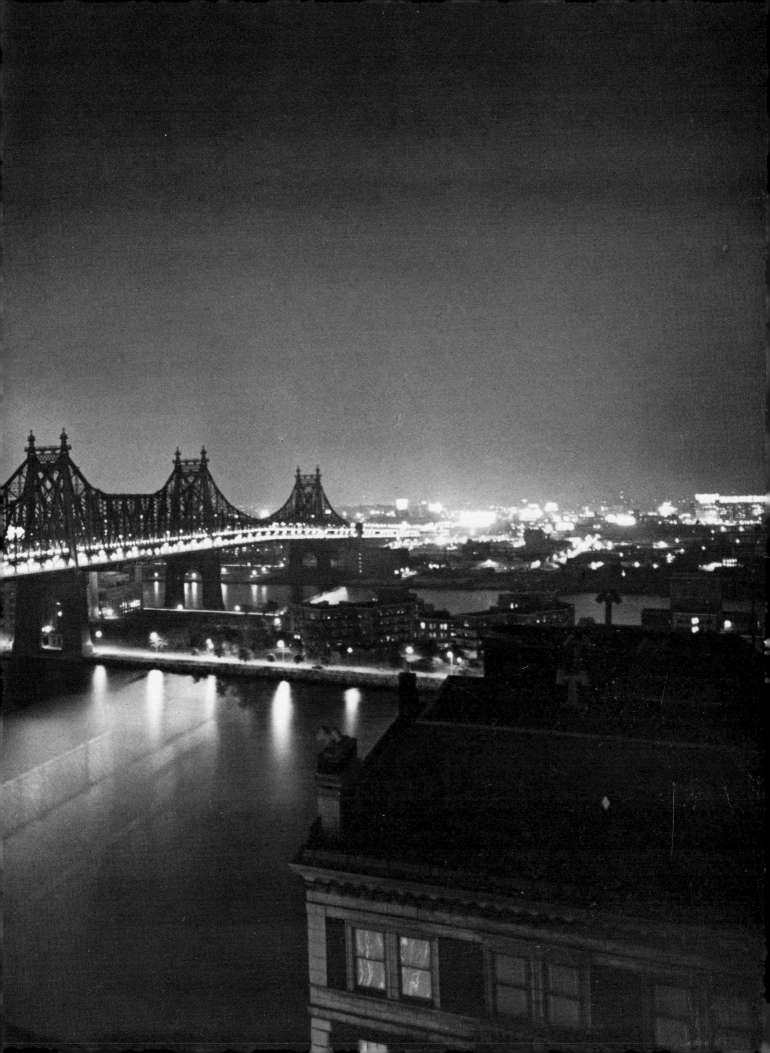

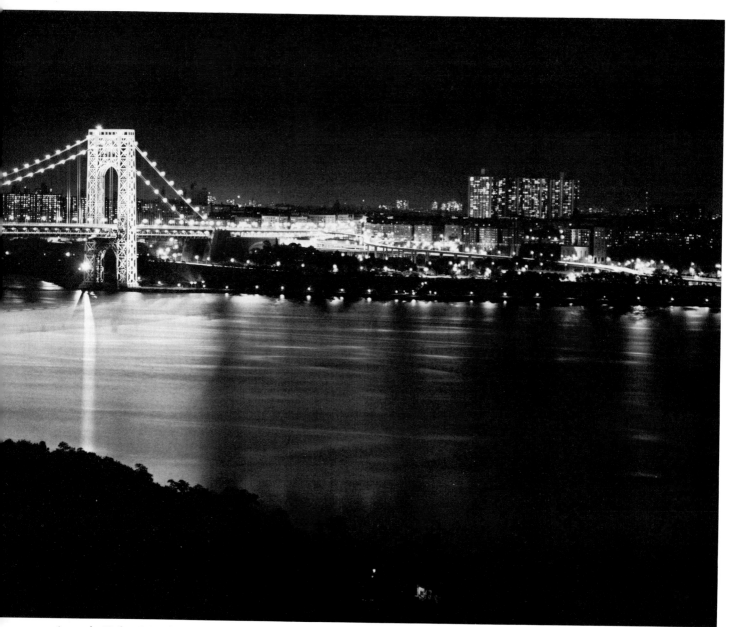

Across the Hudson River from New Jersey toward Washington Heights;
the George Washington Bridge at left.

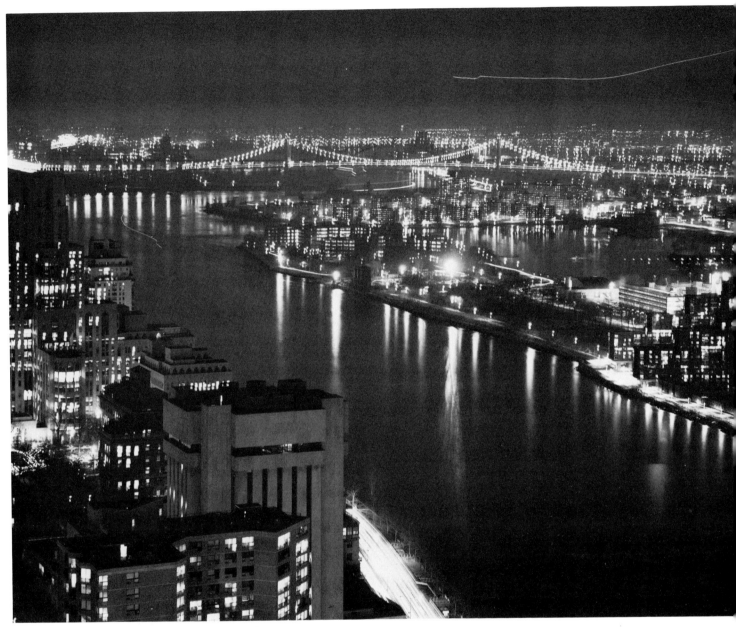

The East River, toward the Triborough Bridge, from the East 60s.

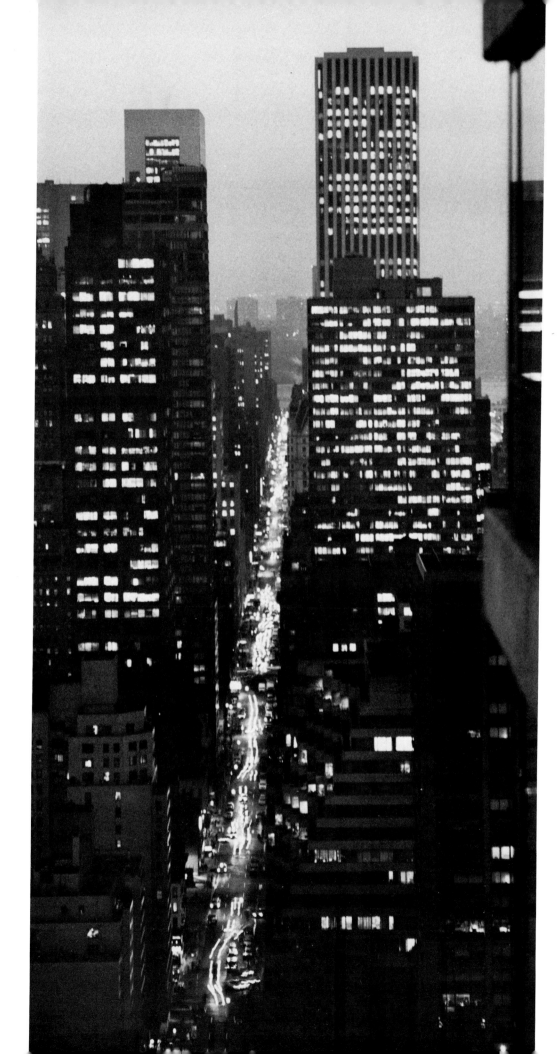

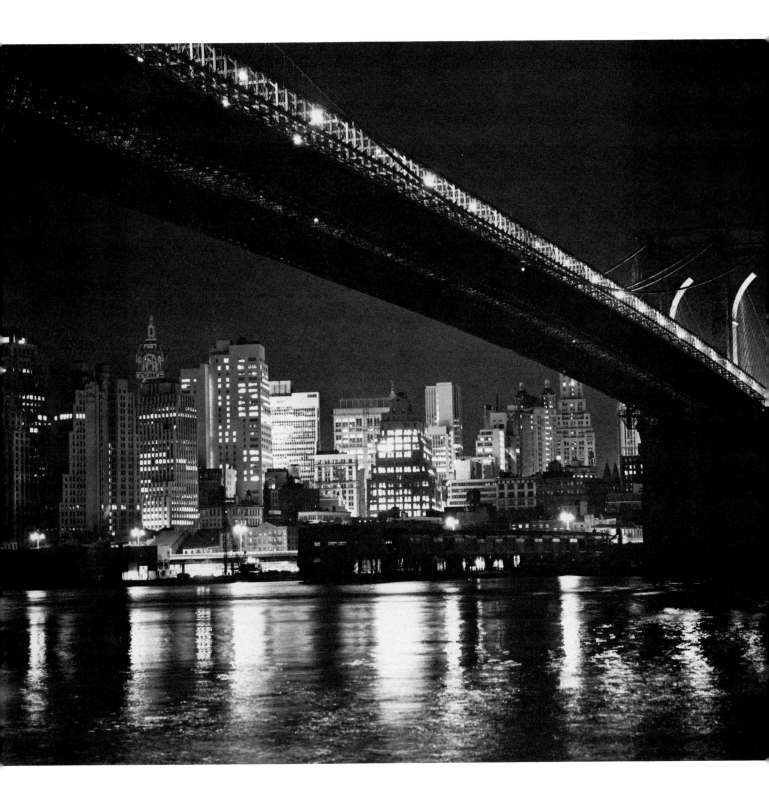

Opposite: West on East 58th Street.
Above: The Brooklyn Bridge from Brooklyn.
Overleaf: North up the East River toward Roosevelt Island and the Queensboro (59th Street) Bridge.

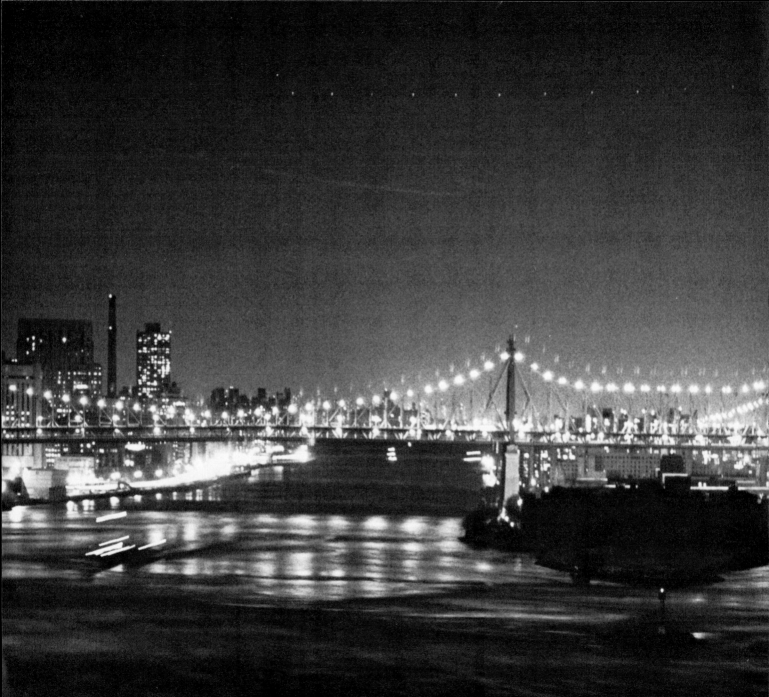

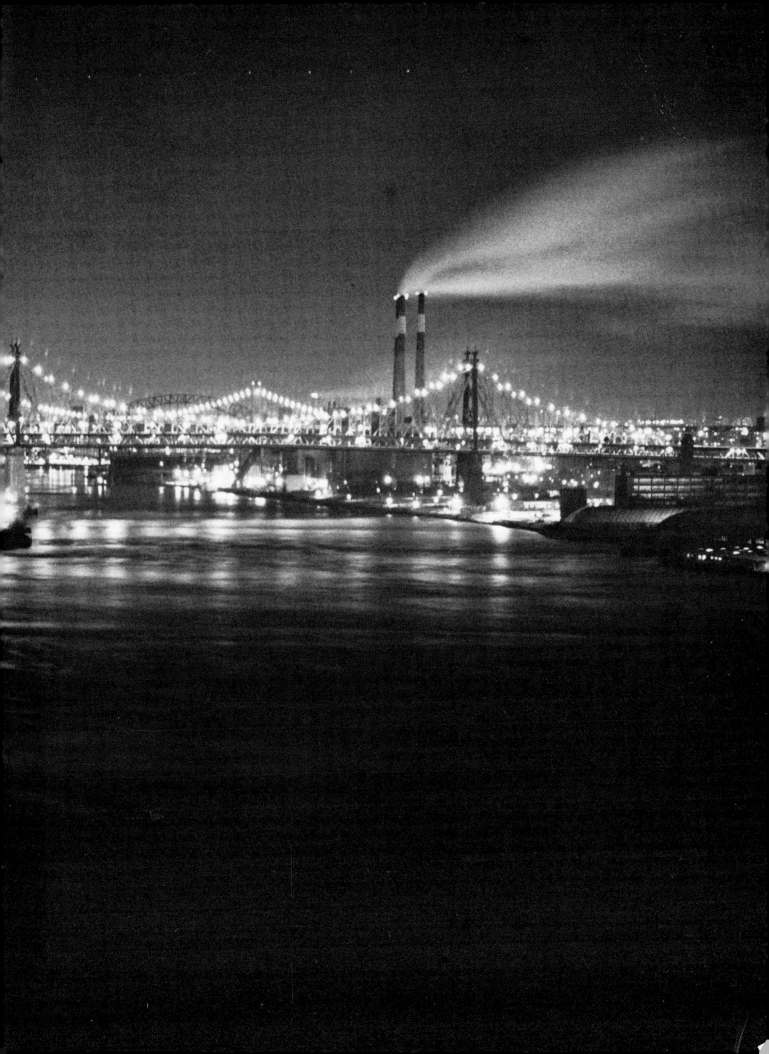

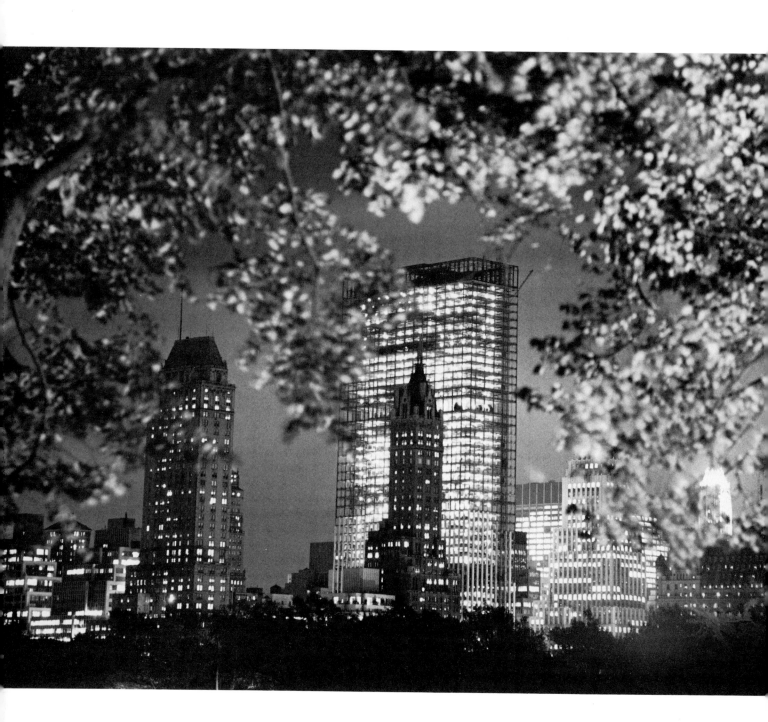

Above and opposite: Southeast across Central Park; the Hotel Pierre at left and the Sherry Netherland Hotel silhouetted against the General Motors Building.
Overleaf: South on the Hudson River to the George Washington Bridge.

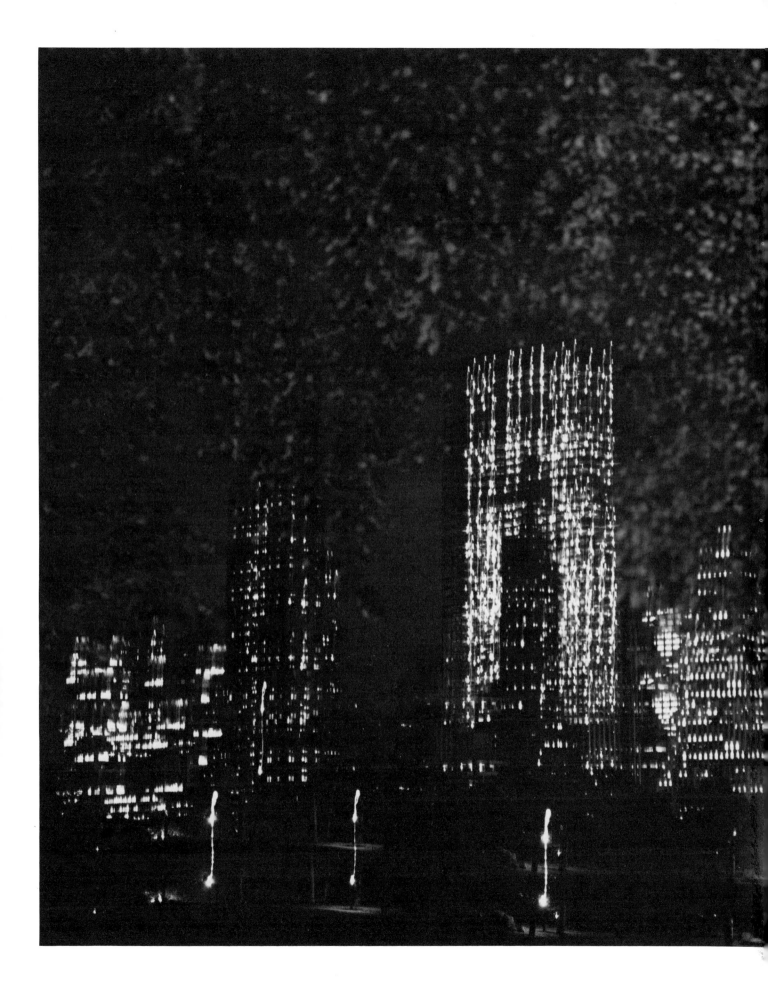

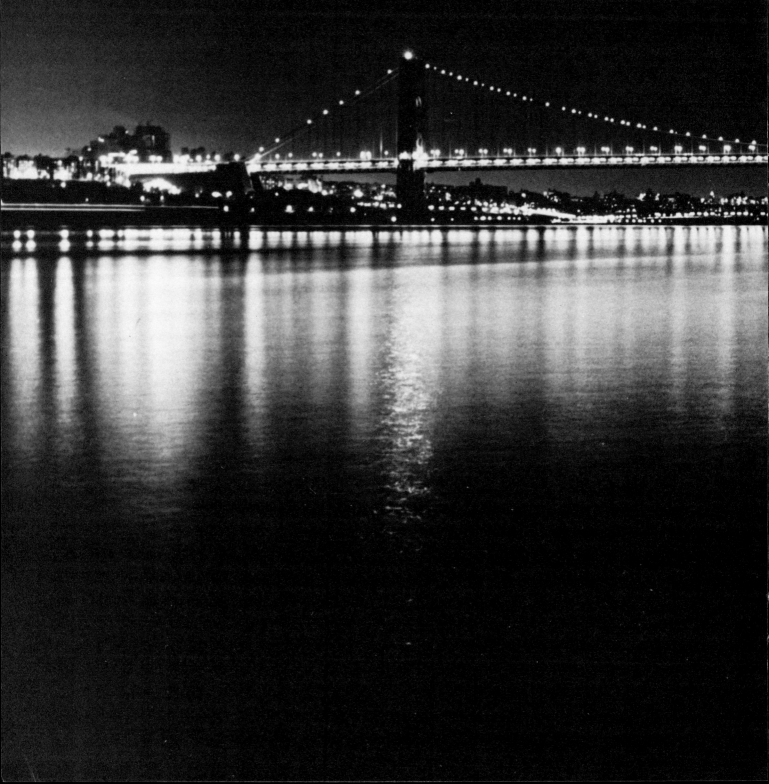

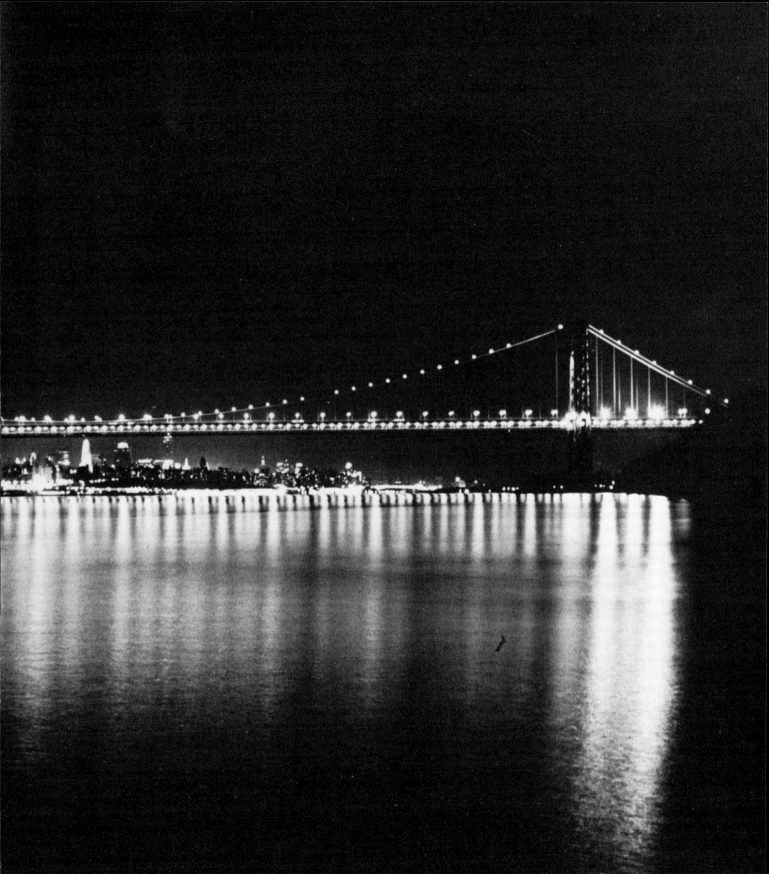

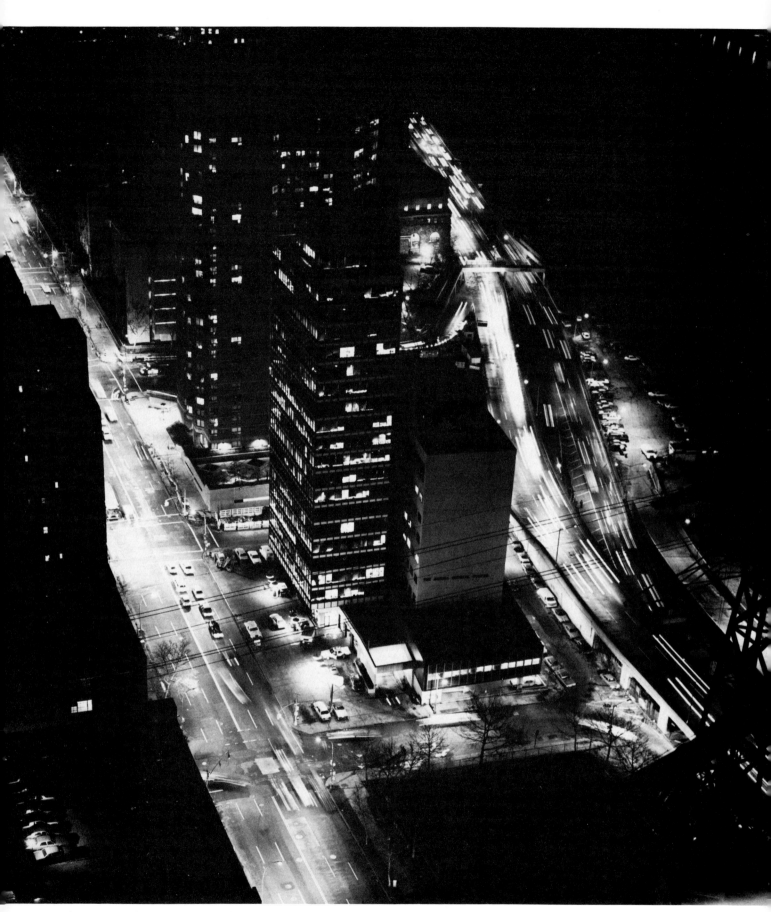

The Animal Medical Center, East 62nd Street at the East River.

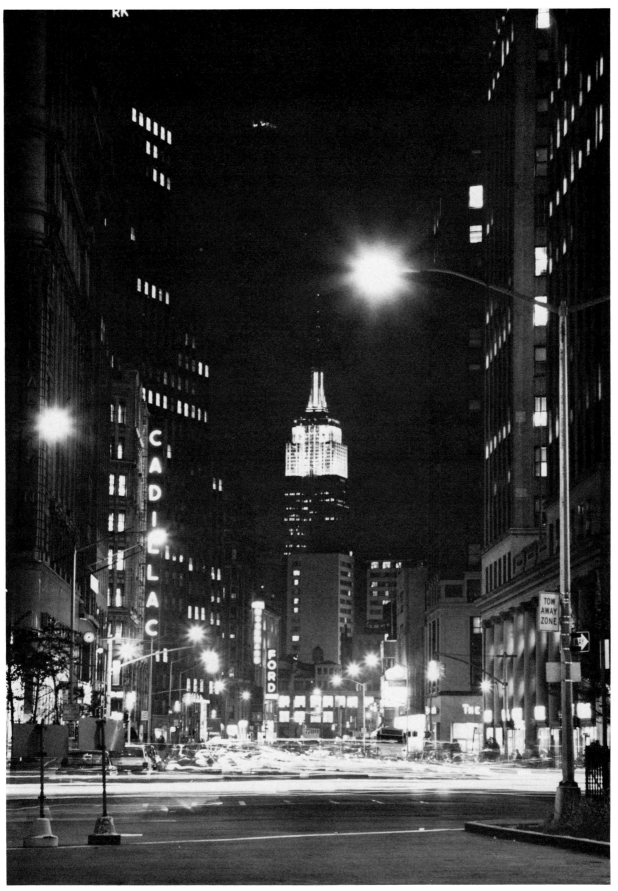

The Empire State Building from Columbus Circle.

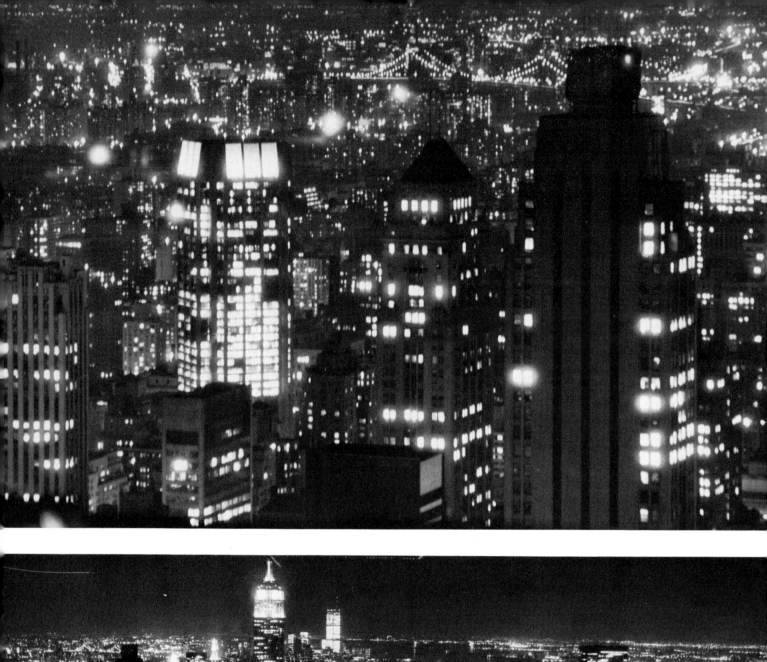

Top: Southeast from the East 30s. *Bottom:* South from the RCA Building.

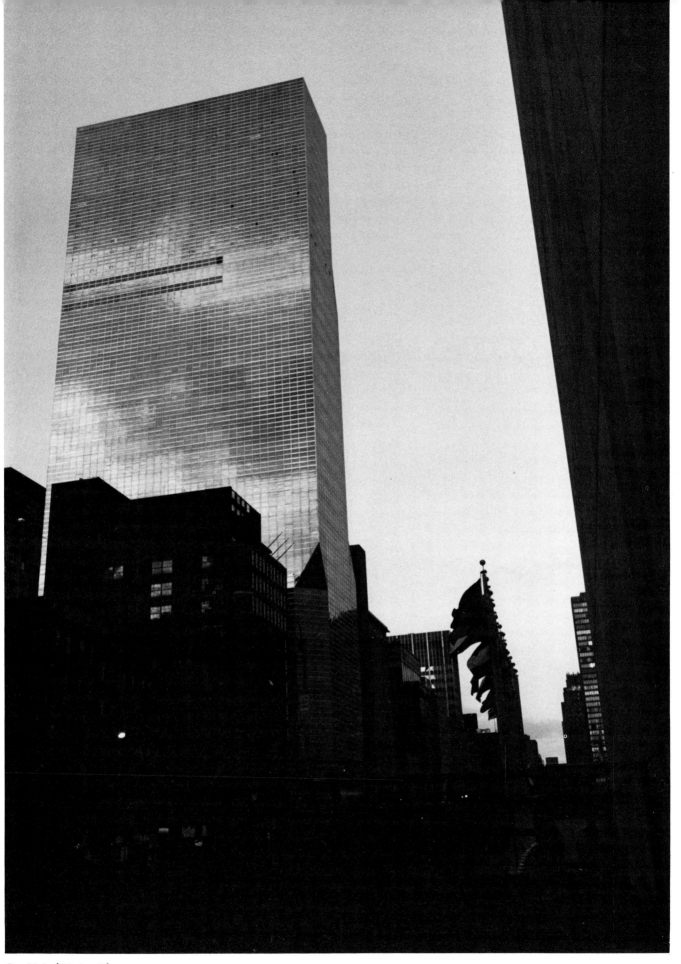

One United Nations Plaza.

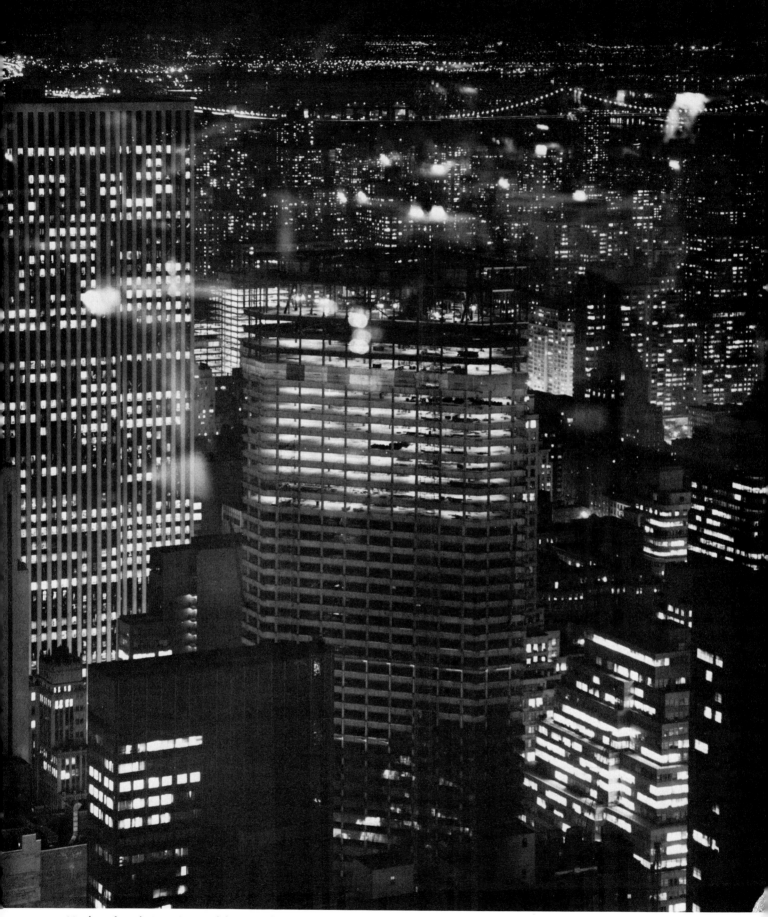

Northeast from the East 40s toward the Queensboro (59th Street) Bridge.

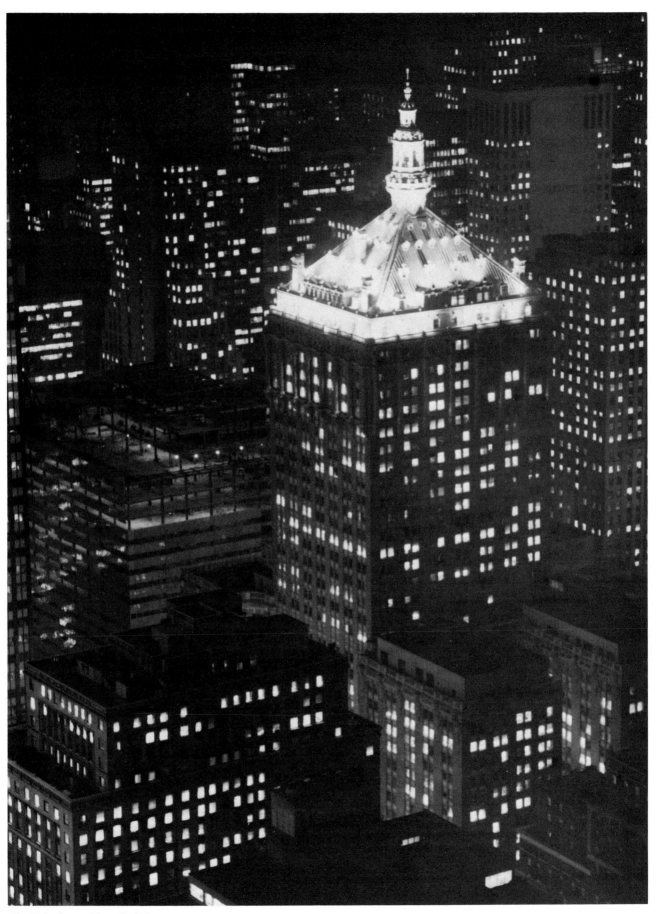

The Helmsley Building, **Park Avenue**.

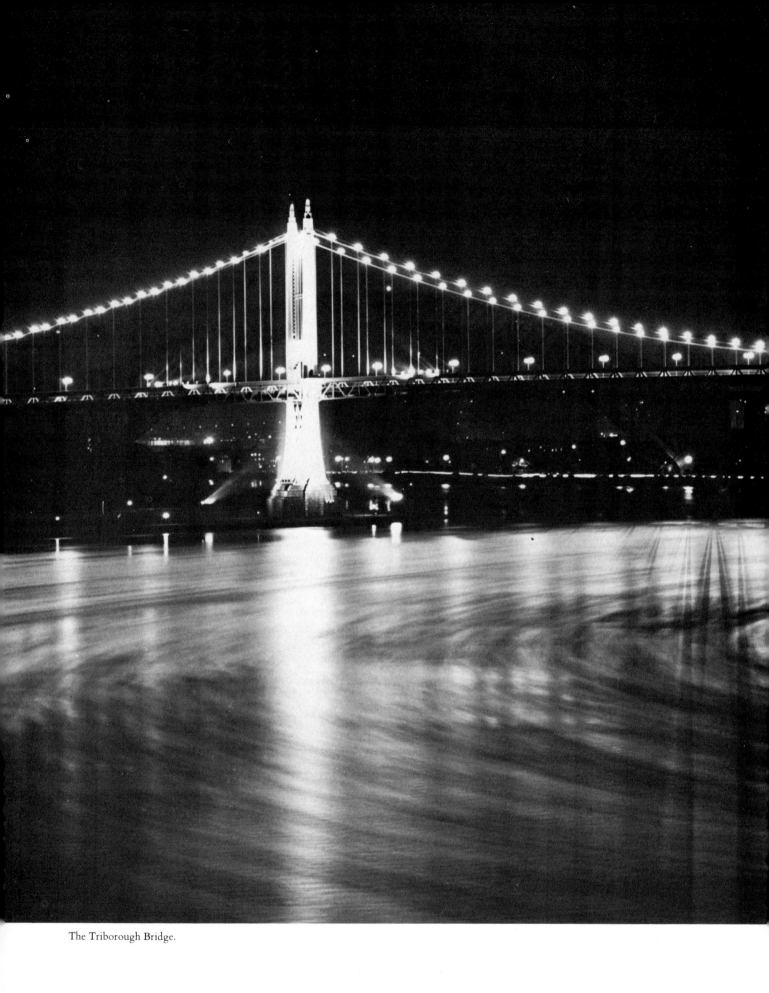

The Triborough Bridge.

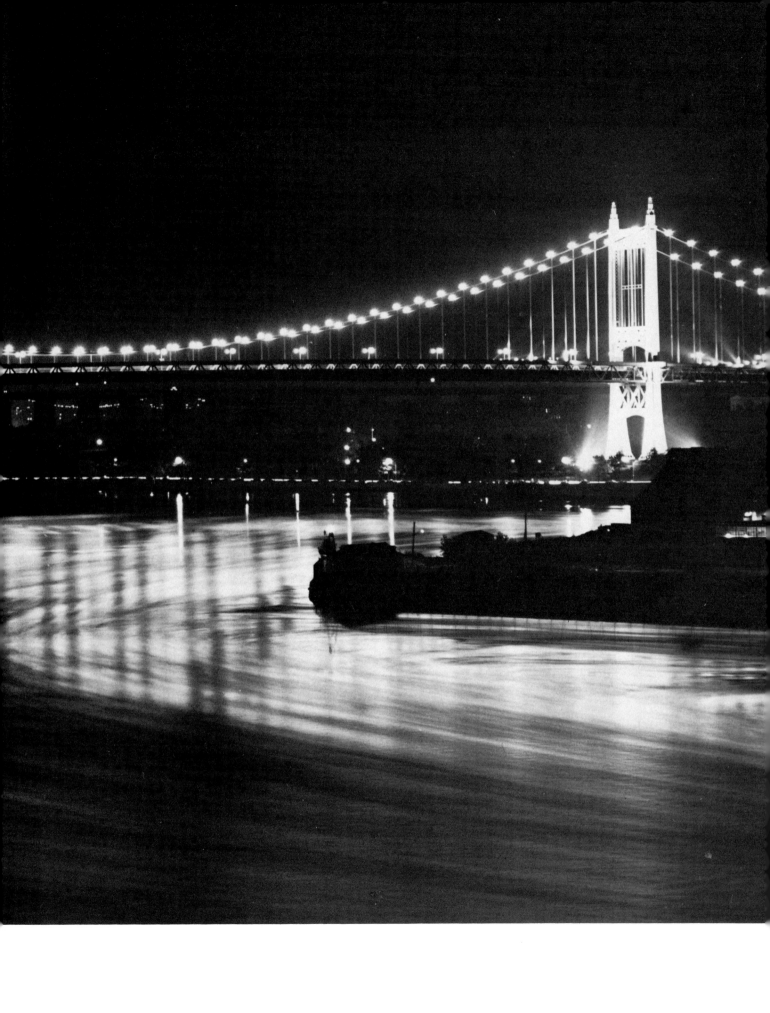

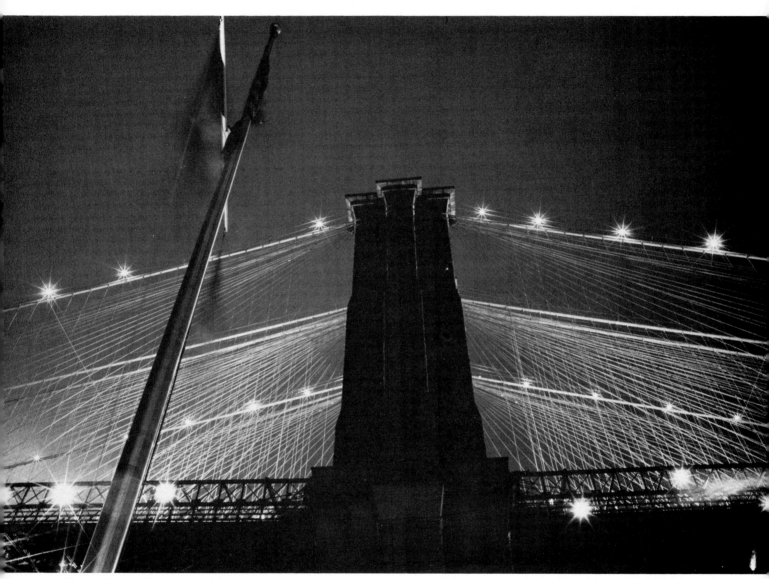

The Brooklyn Bridge.

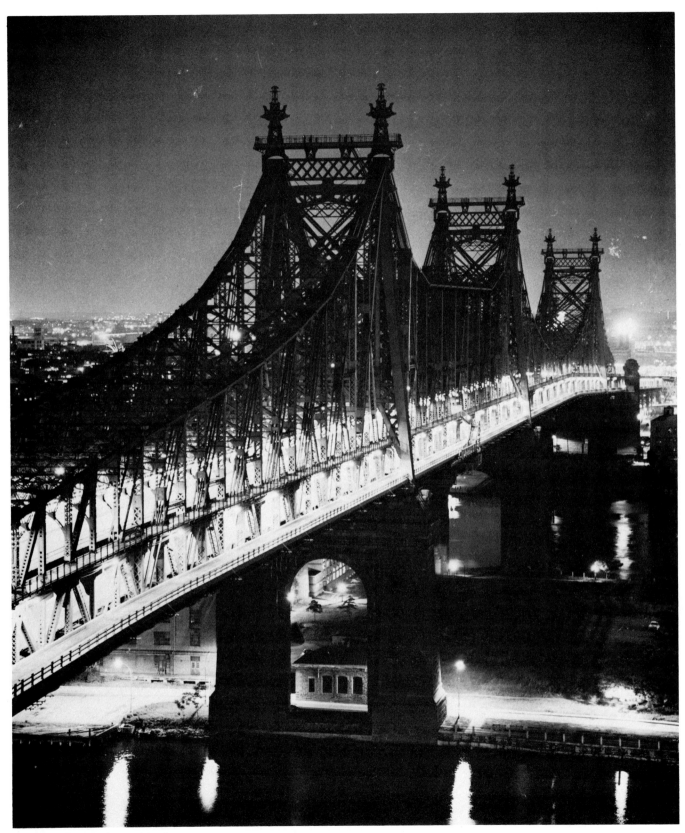

The Queensboro (59th Street) Bridge.

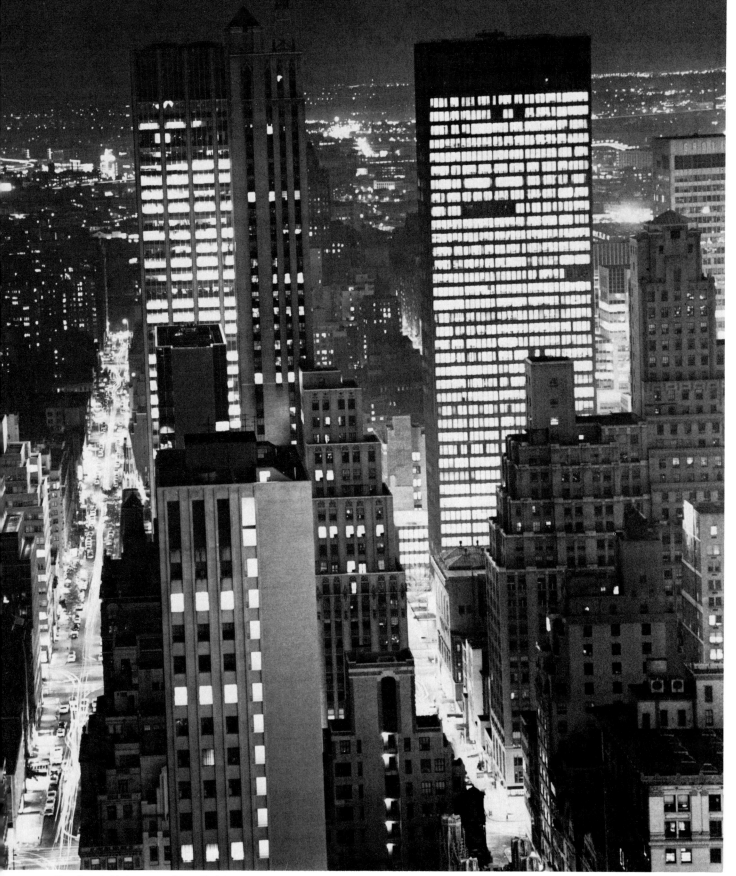

East from Fifth Avenue and East 53rd Street.

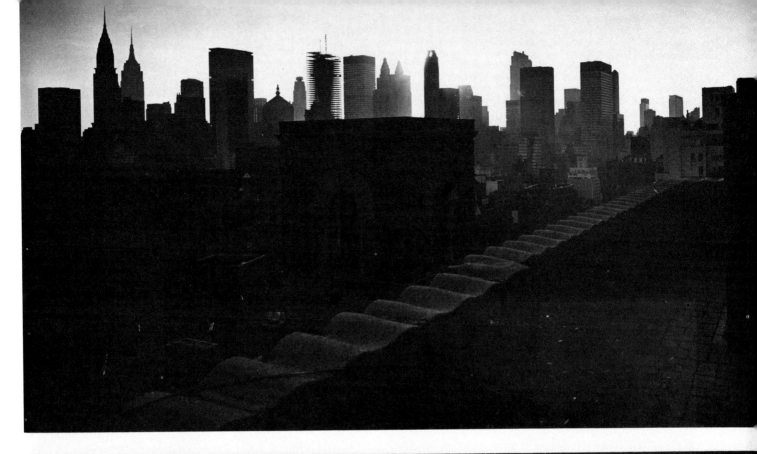

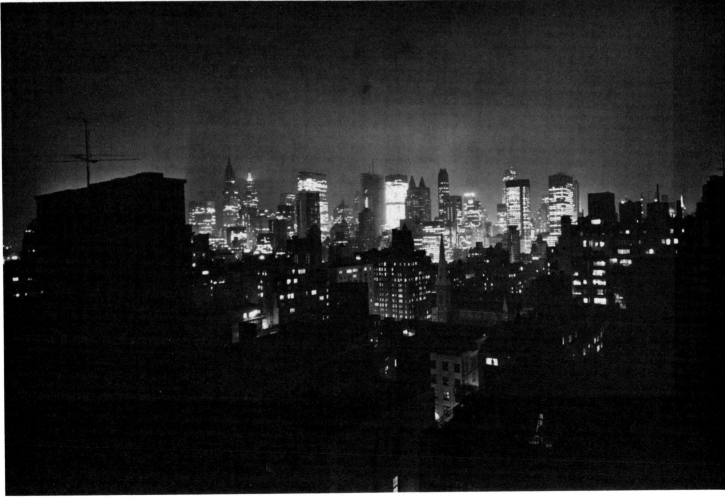

Top, bottom and overleaf: Southwest from the East 50s.

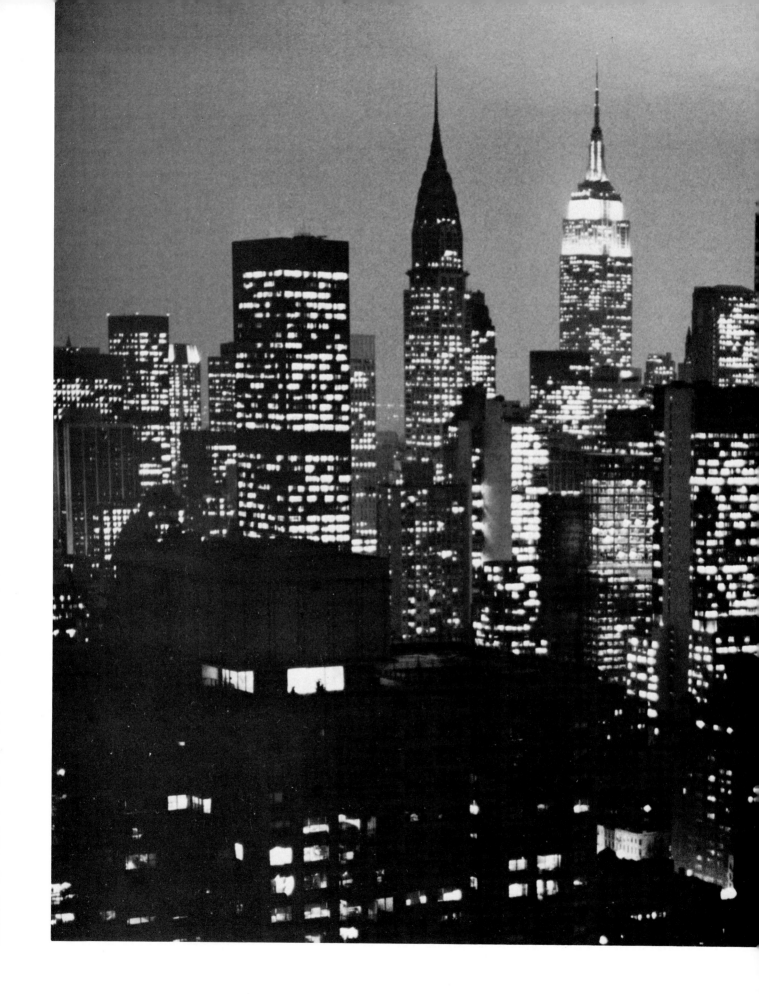

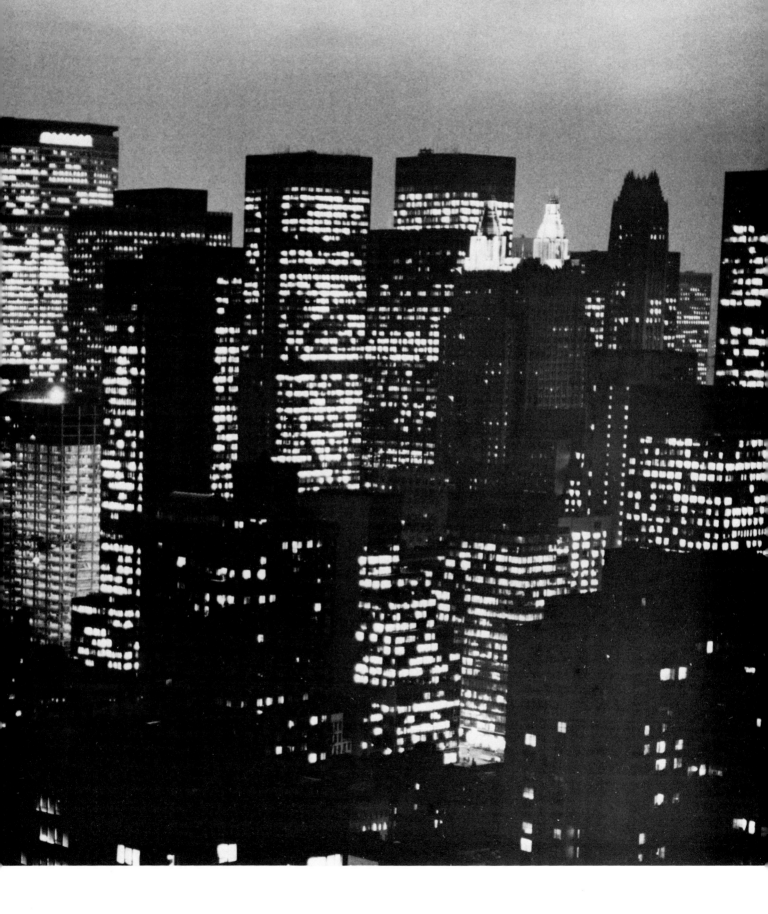

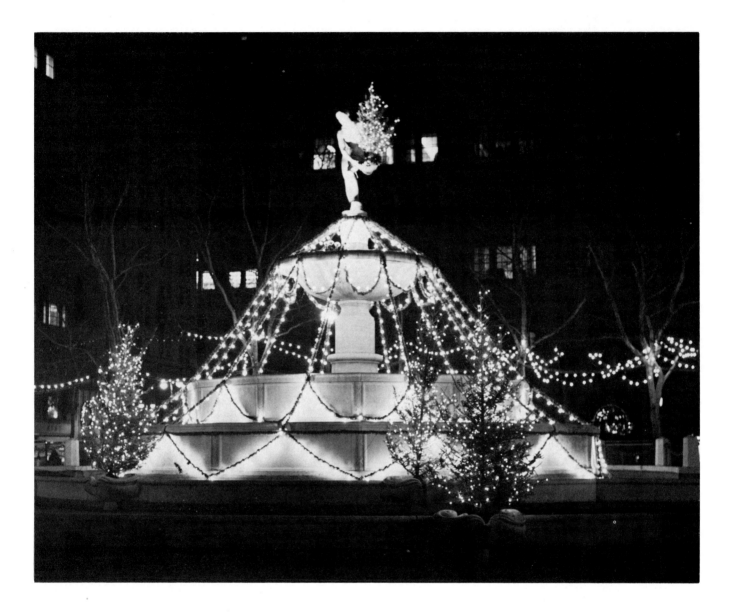

Above: The Pulitzer Fountain, Grand Army Plaza. *Opposite:* South from Third Avenue in the East 40s; Chrysler Building at left, Pan Am Building at right.

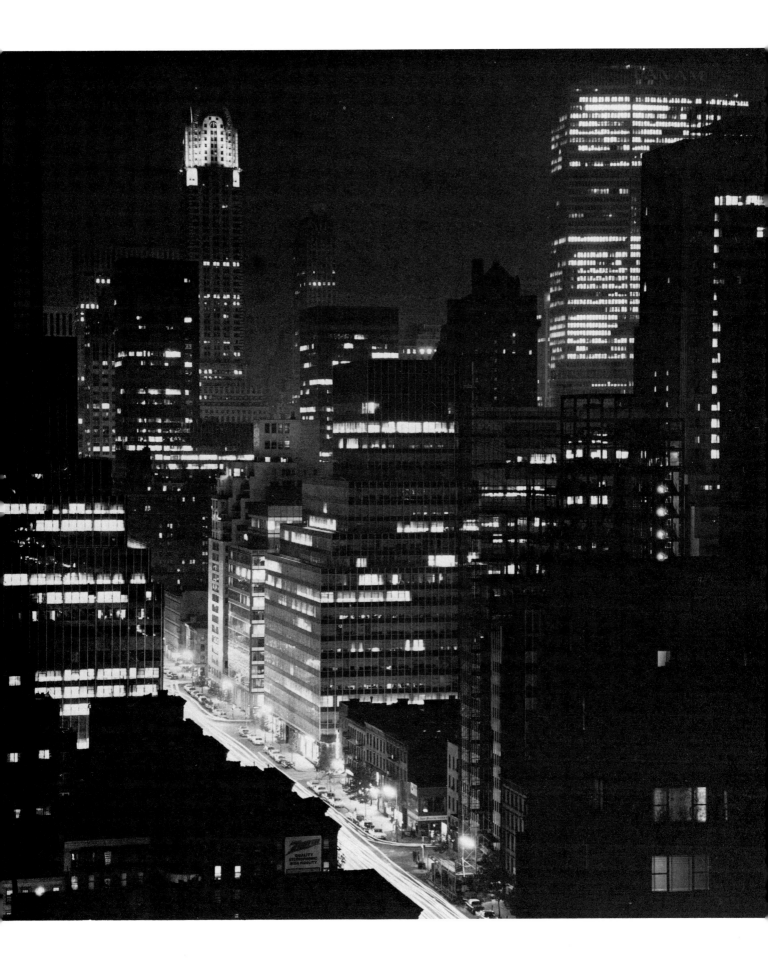

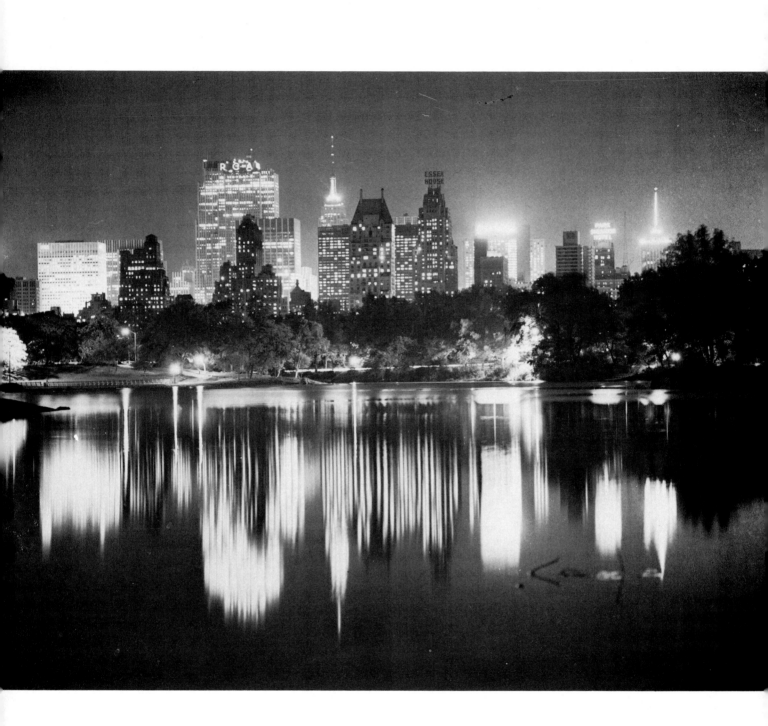

Above: South from the Lake, Central Park.
Opposite: The Empire State Building.

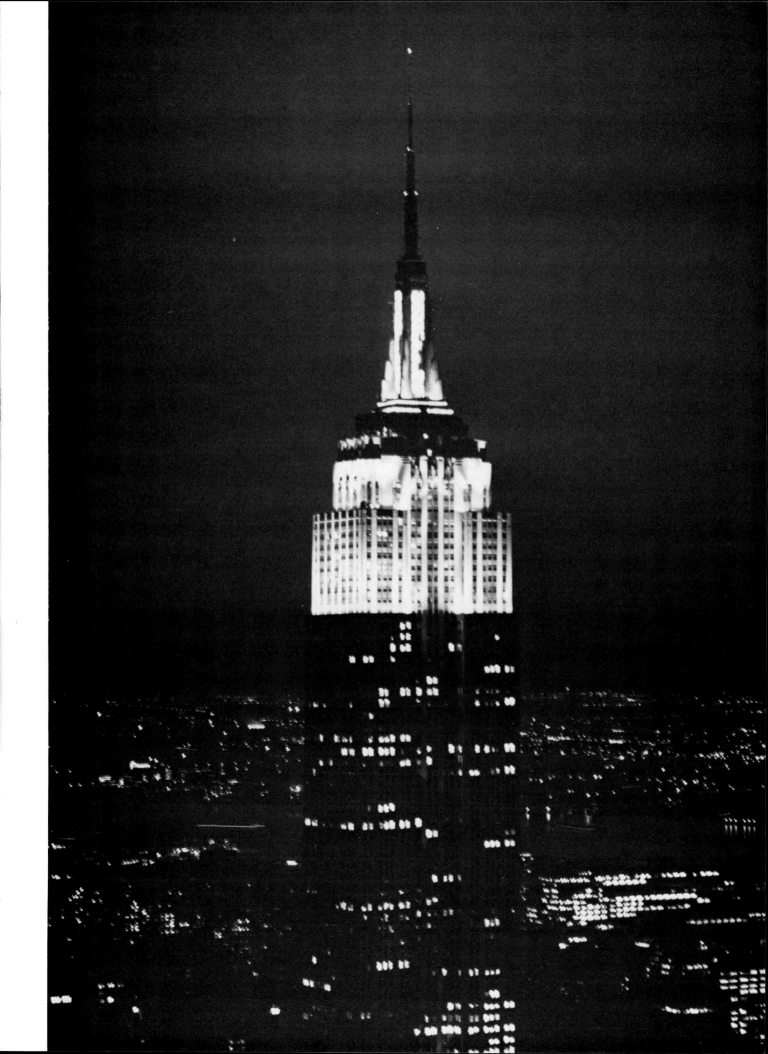

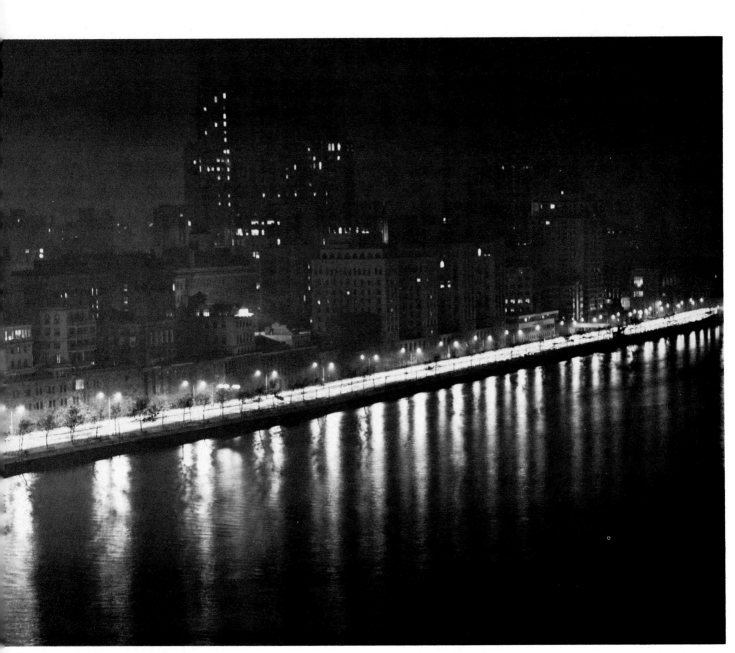

The East River Drive in the East 60s.

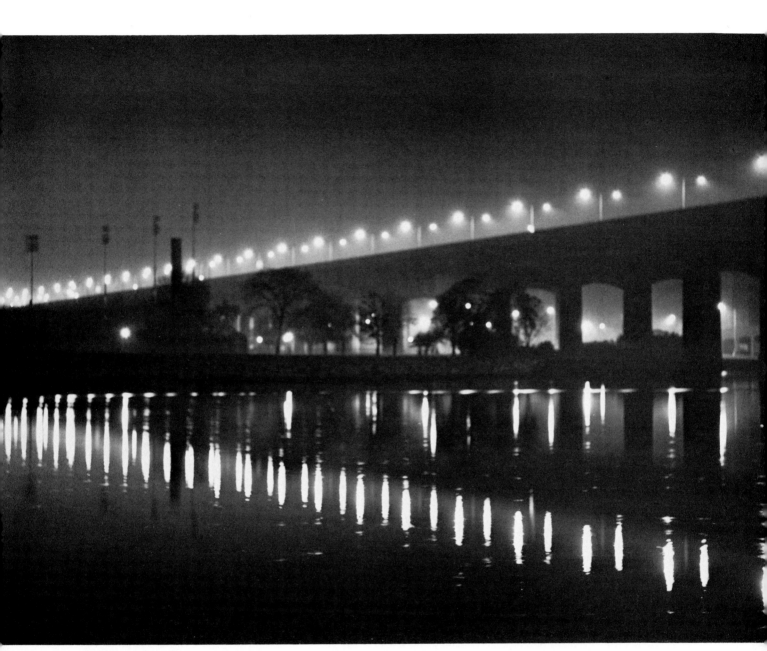

Above: The Triborough Bridge.
Overleaf: The Harlem River.

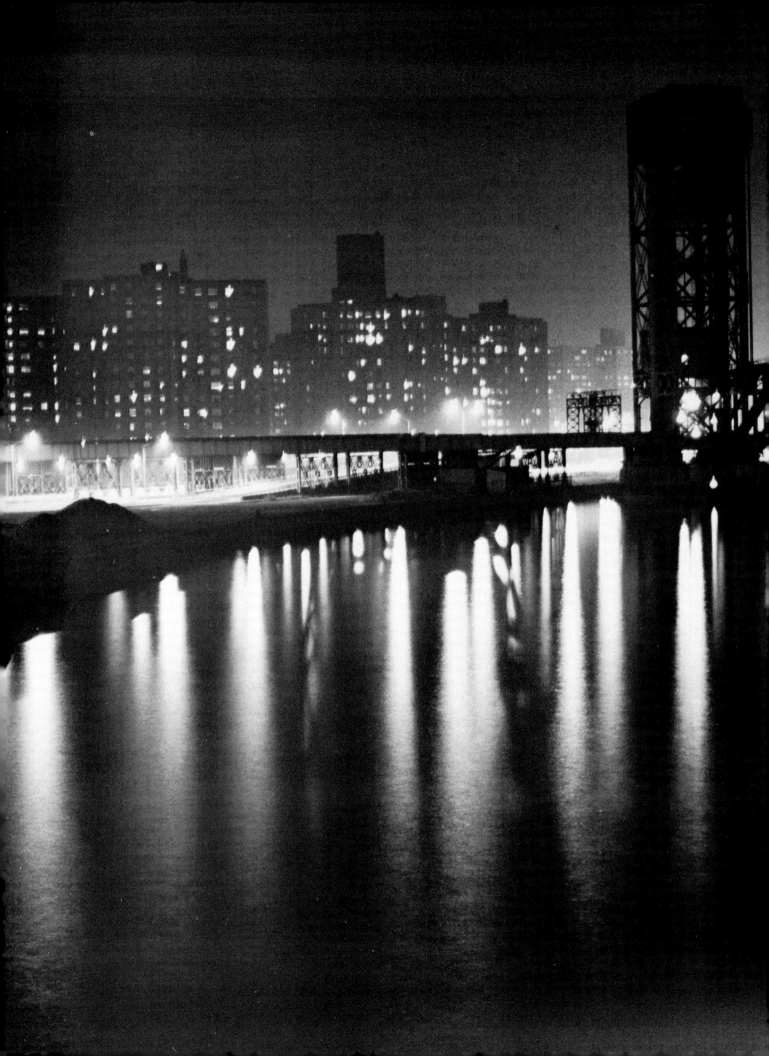

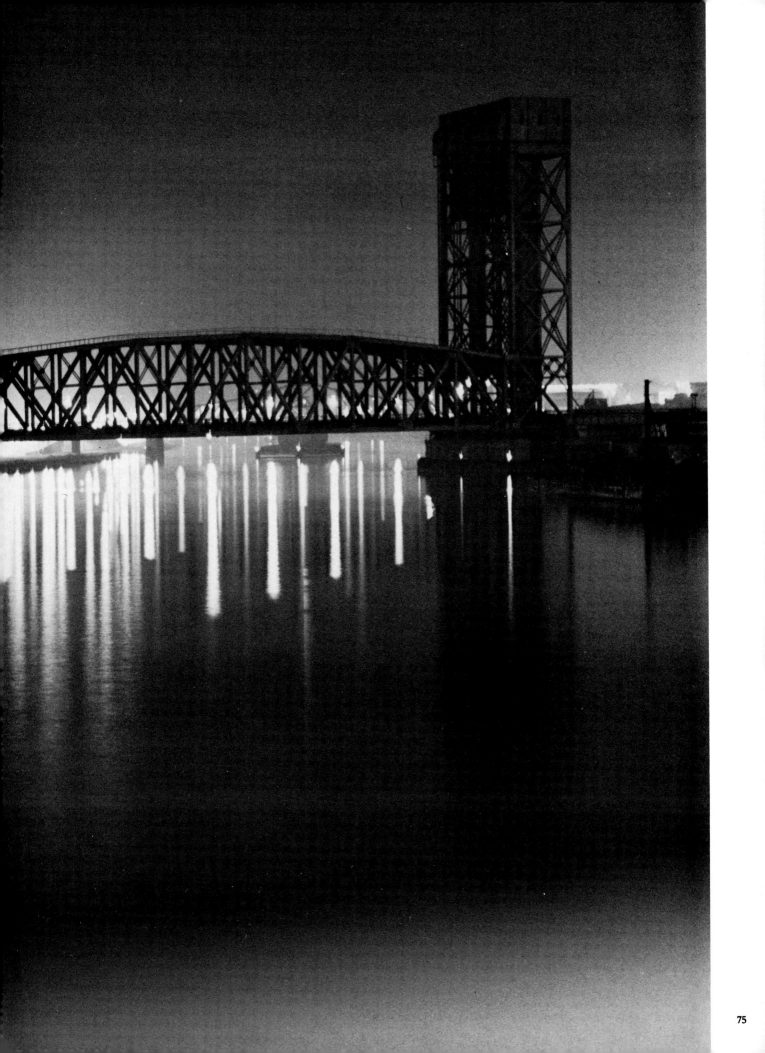

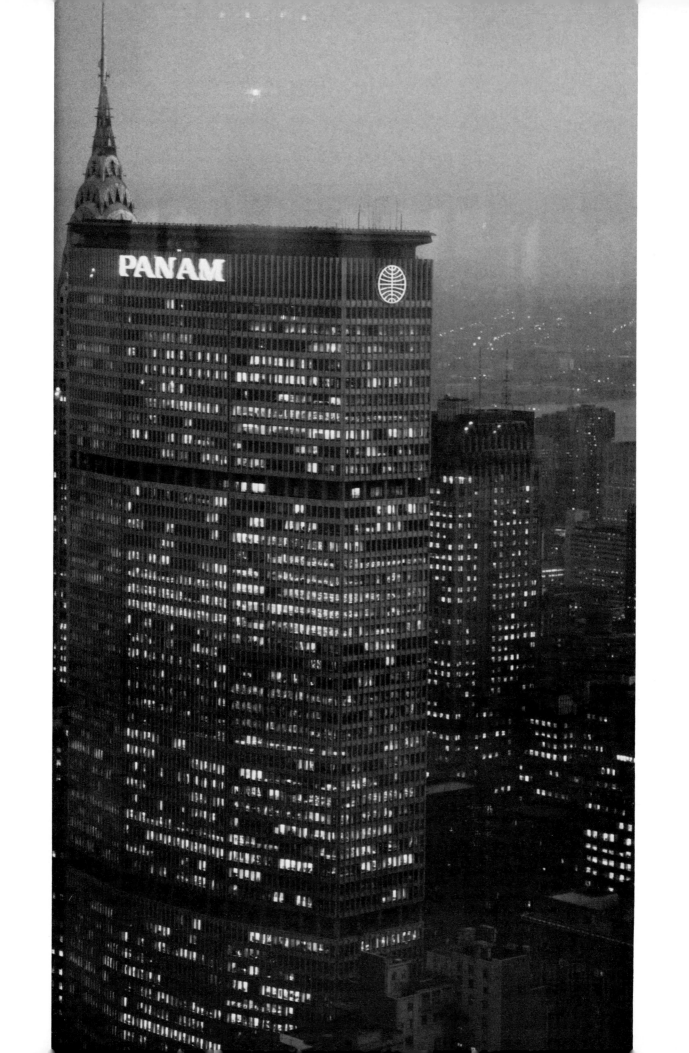

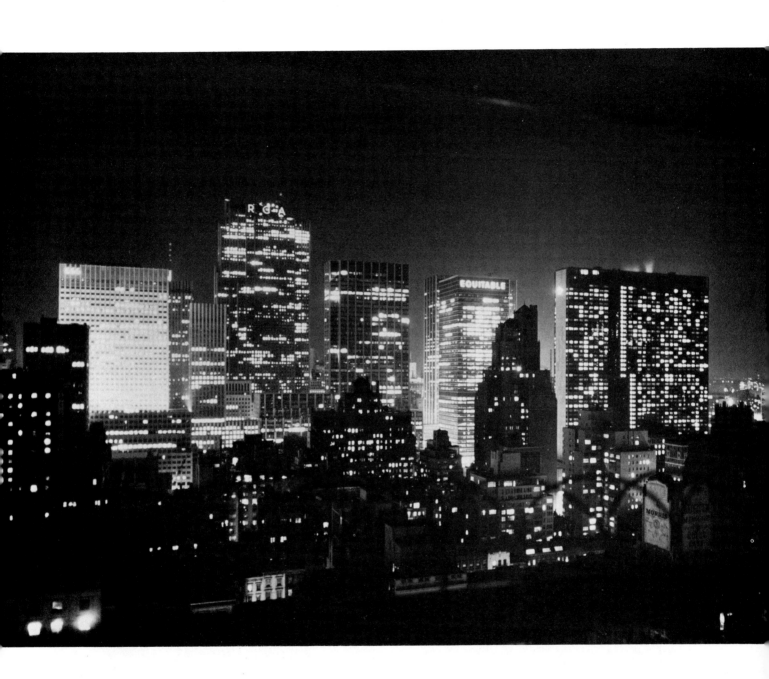

Opposite: The Pan Am Building. *Above:* South from the West 50s.

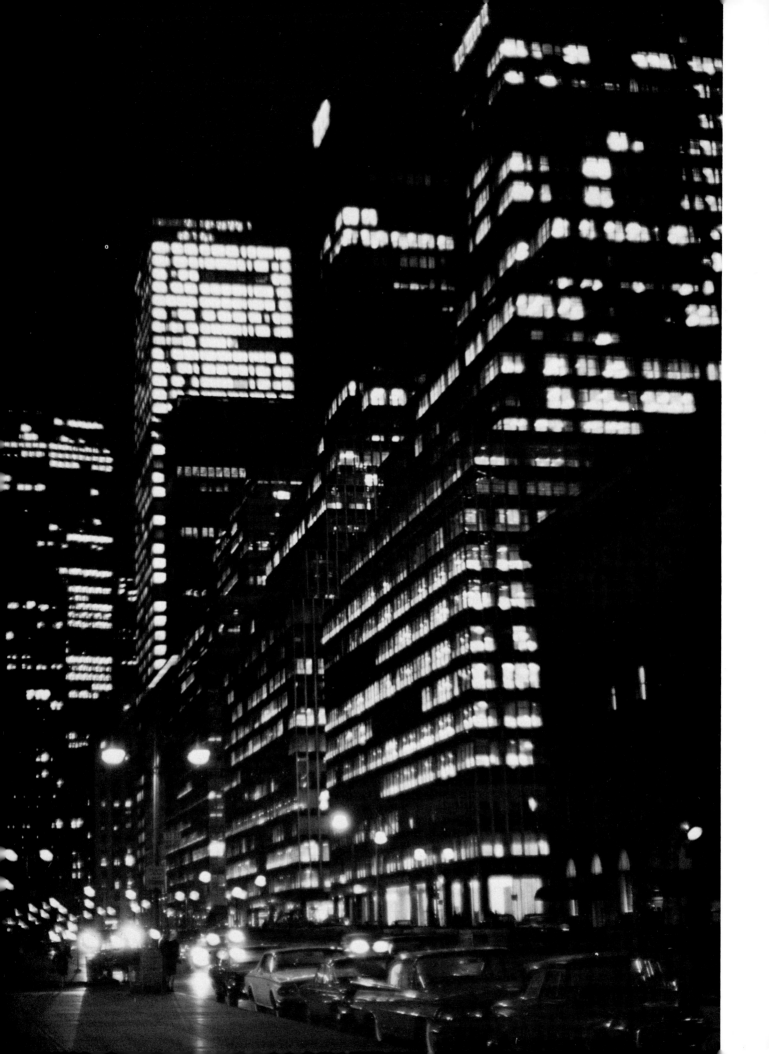

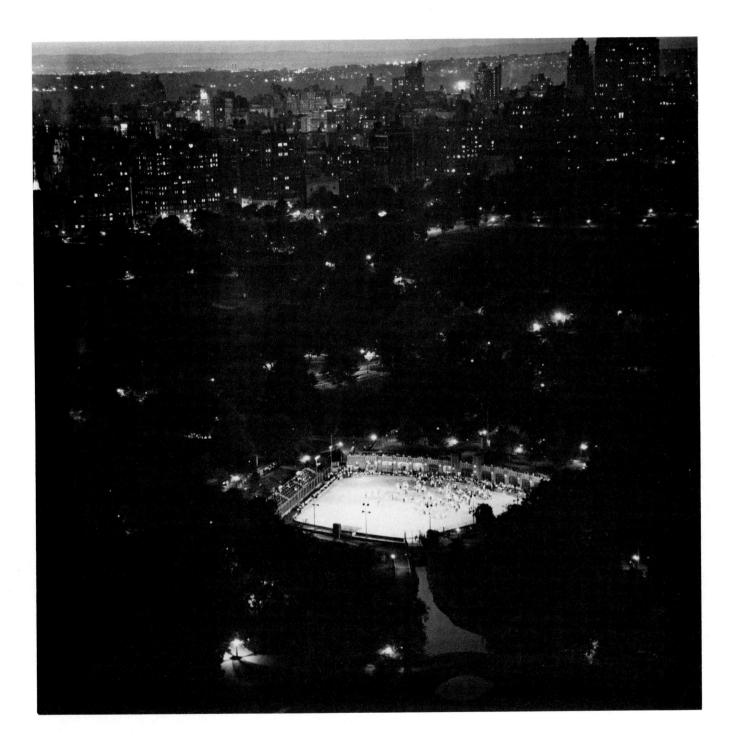

Opposite: Park Avenue, south from East 53rd Street.
Above: Wollman Memorial Rink, Central Park.

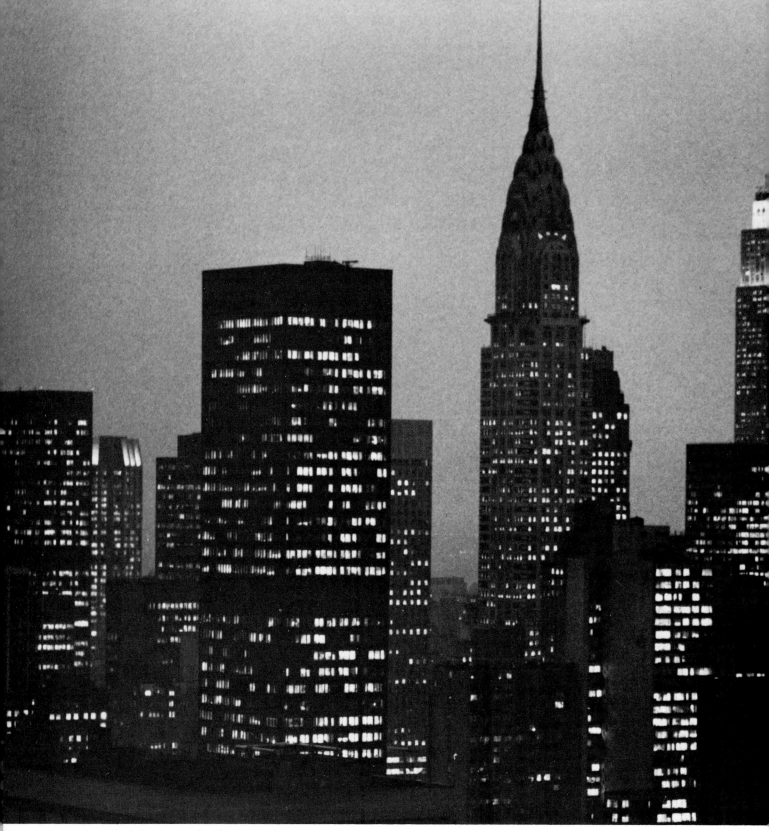

Southwest from the East 50s; the Chrysler Building at left, the Empire State Building at center and the Pan Am Building at right.

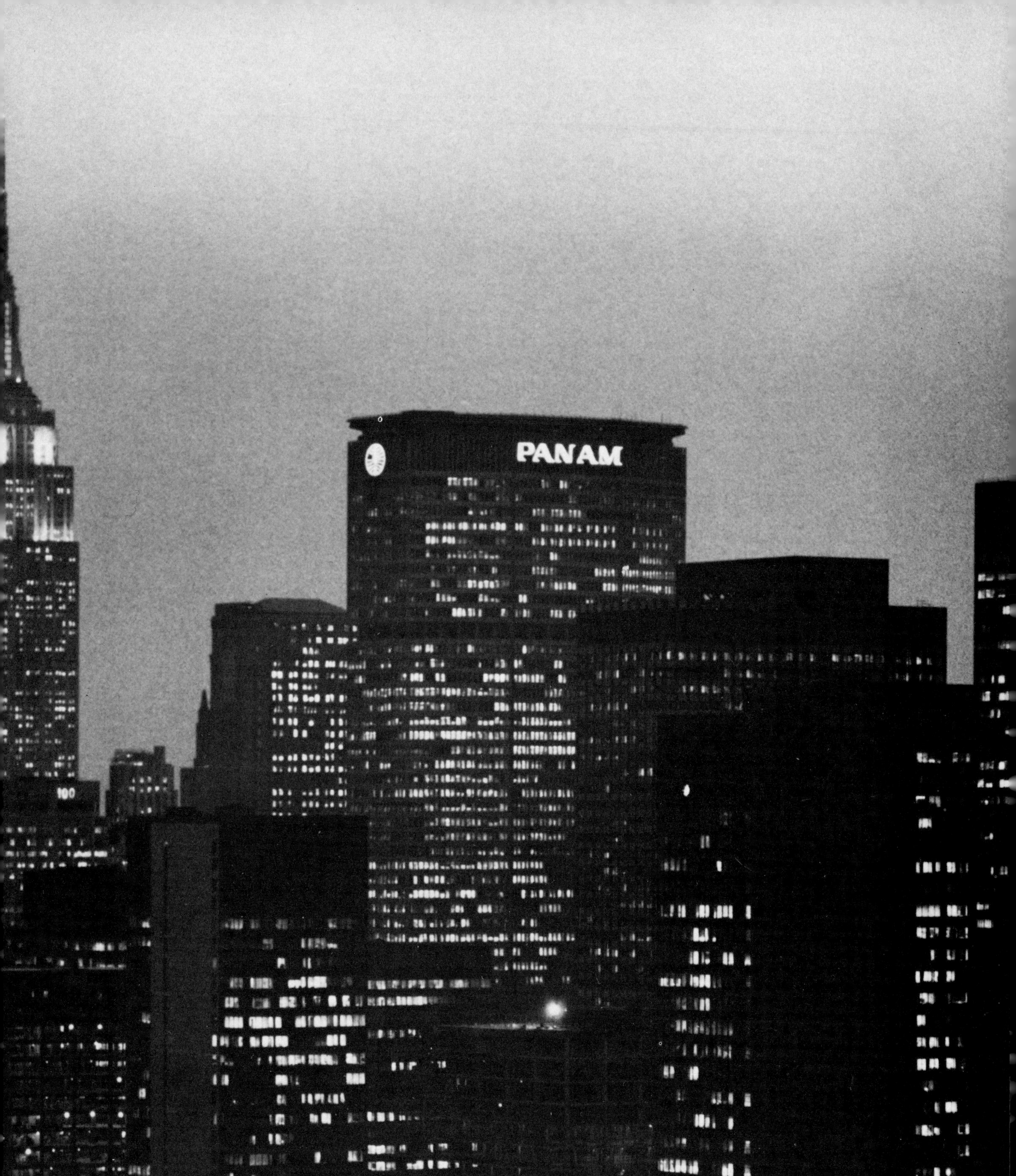
PAN AM

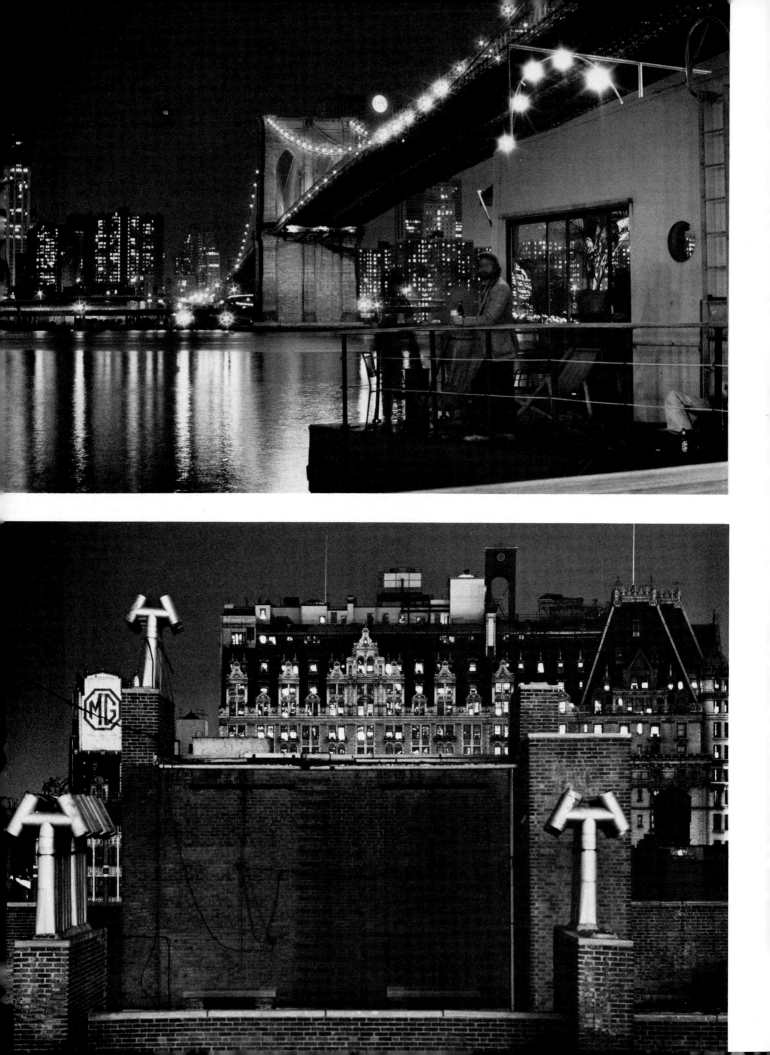

Opposite, top: The Brooklyn Bridge from the River Café, Brooklyn.
Opposite, bottom: The Plaza Hotel. *Above:* 9 West 57th Street.
Overleaf: South from East 58st Street.

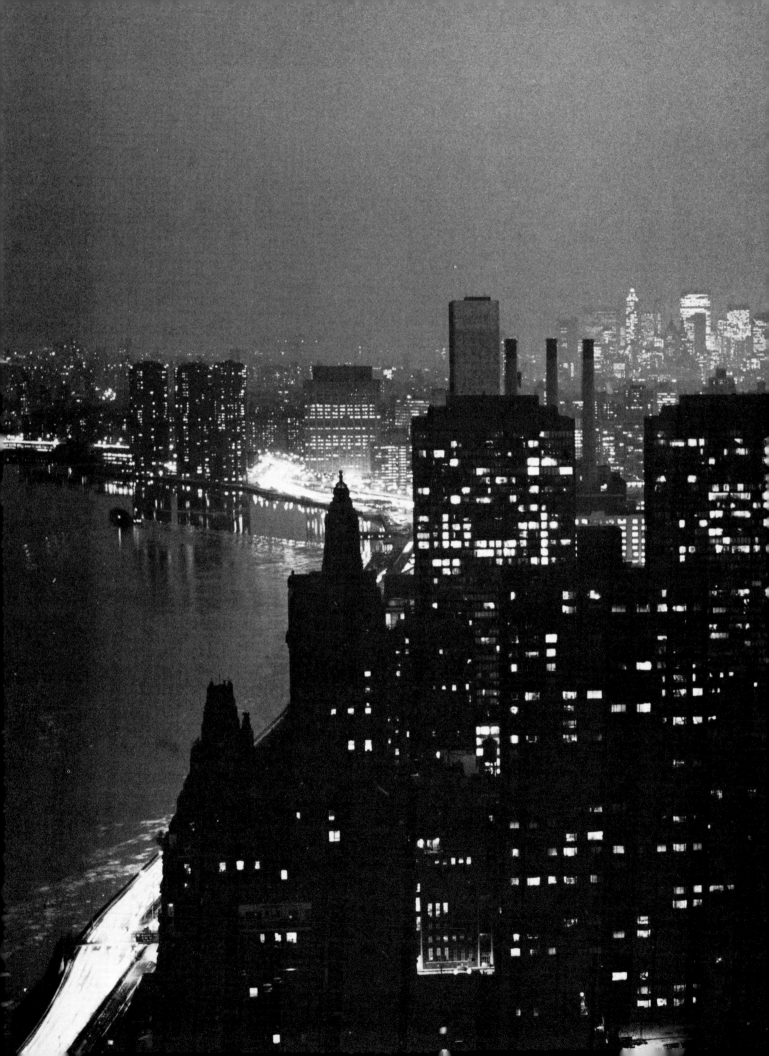

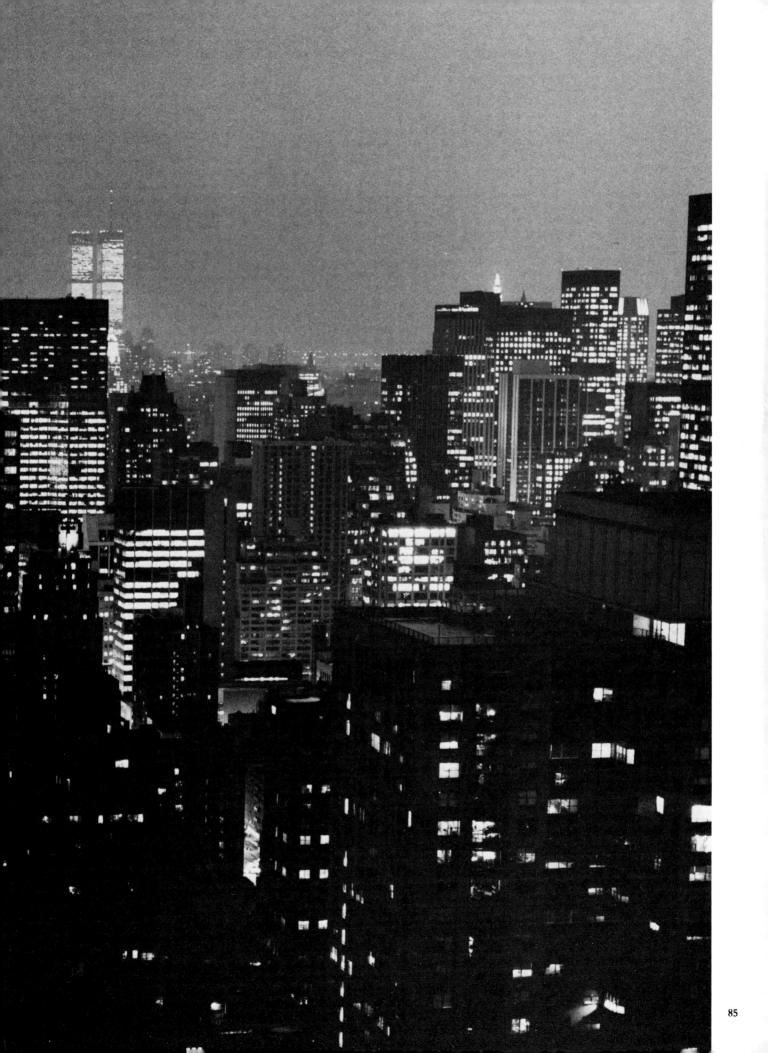

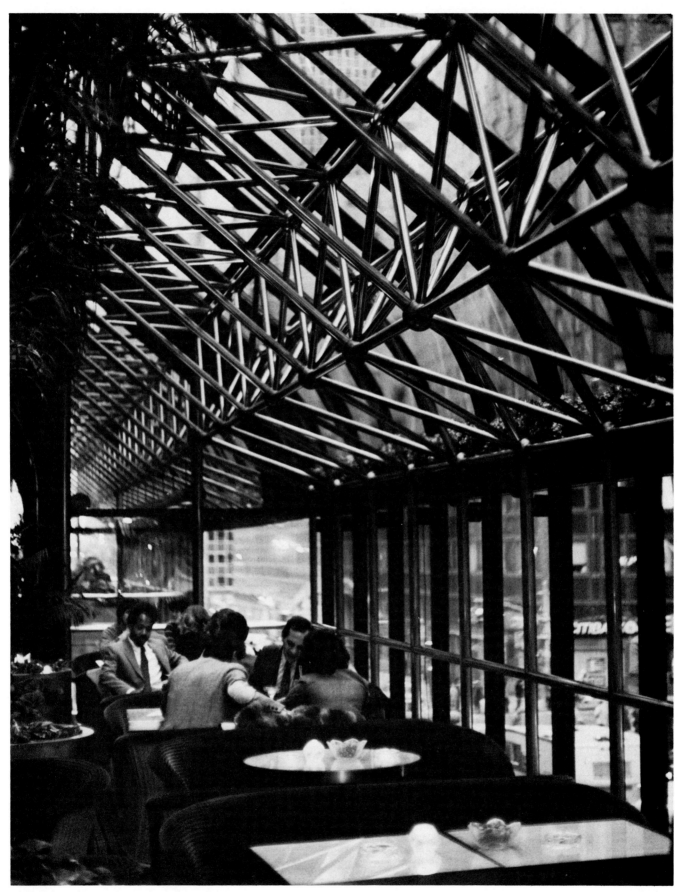

Cocktail bar, the Grand Hyatt Hotel, East 42nd Street and Lexington Avenue.

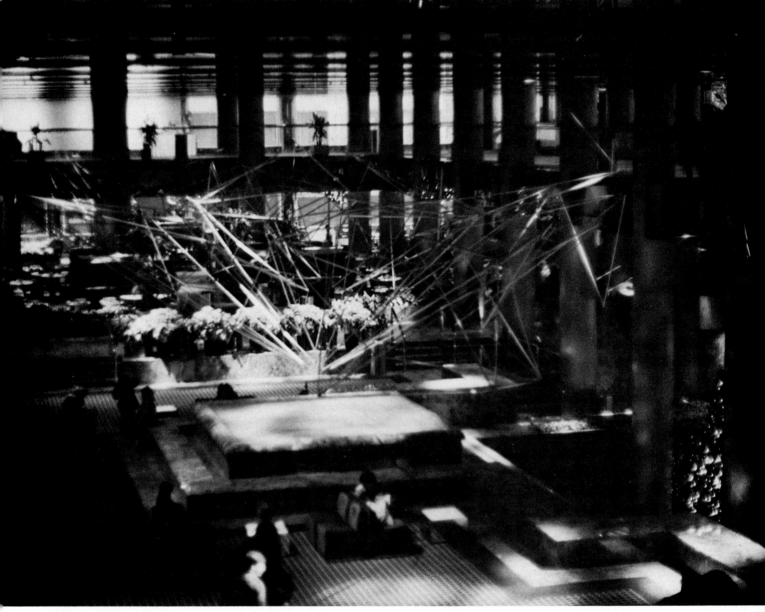

Lobby, the Grand Hyatt Hotel.

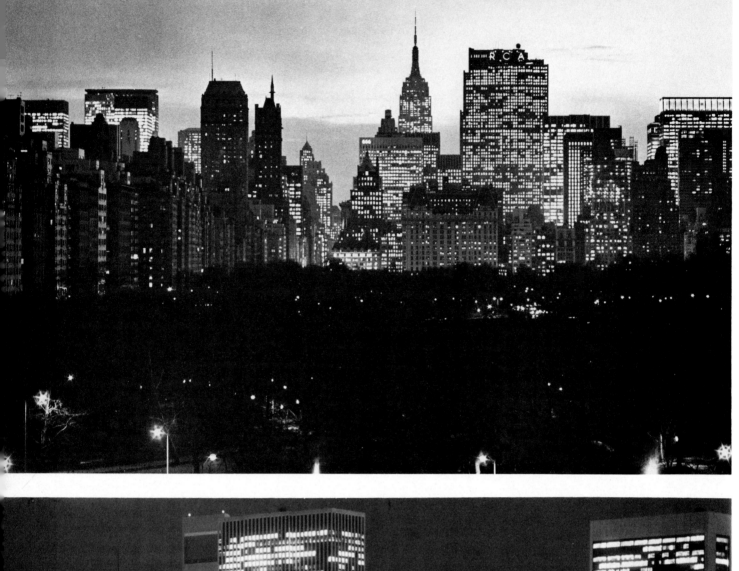

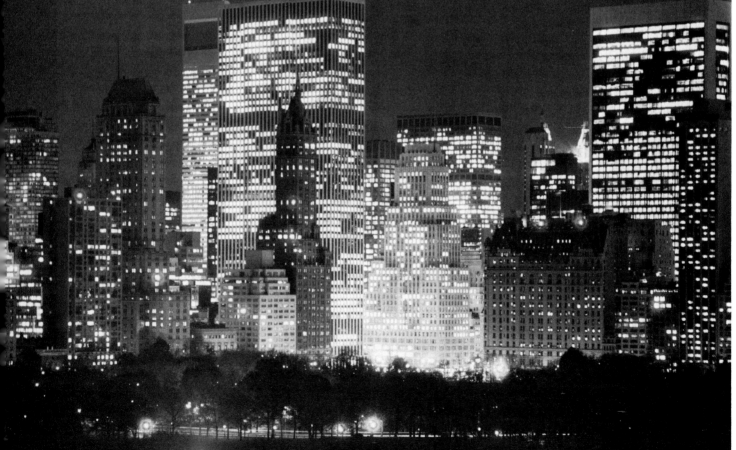

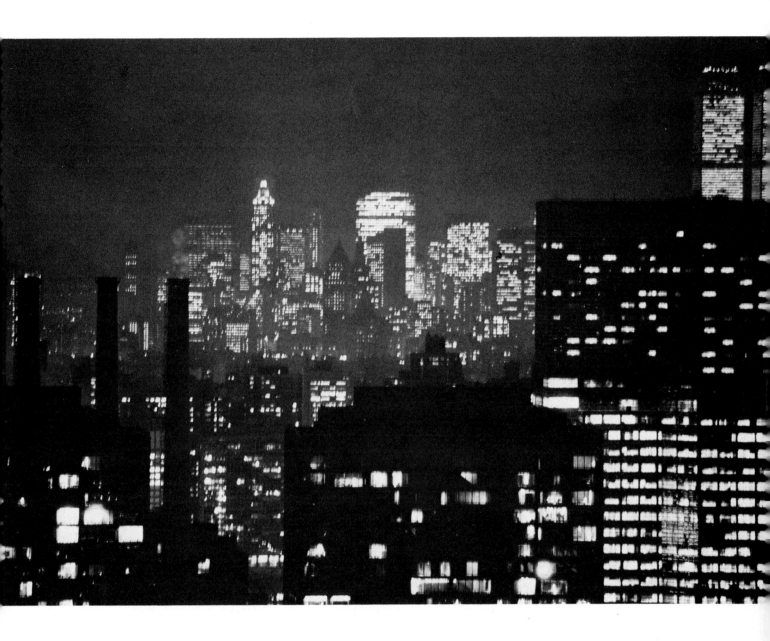

Opposite, top: South from Central Park, near Fifth Avenue in the 70s.
Opposite, bottom: Southeast across Central Park. *Above:* South from East
58th Street.